KU-544-347

Contents

Acknowledgements

In the spirit of this book I'm not going to just acknowledge people; I want to share with you who has had an IMPACT in my life and who has allowed this dream of mine to come to fruition.

My parents. These are the people who obviously had the first IMPACT on my life and gave me both the DNA and emotional support I needed to succeed in helping people to realize their dreams. The blend of my solid, dependable father who showed me the rights and wrongs of the world and the colourfulness and eccentricity of my mother was a magical combination.

My older brother, Andrew Risner. The one person who has never been afraid to tell me when I'm off course.

Fran. My wife; the person who has stood by my side for the last 25 years and has never stopped loving me regardless of what I've done.

My son, Daniel. An amazing young man who every day inspires me in his determination and persistence; one to never follow the crowd and always happy to be true to himself.

My daughter, Sasha. A very special young lady whose beauty is equalled inside and out. A look from her can make or break my day. Thank you for being such an inspiration in my life.

Jack Canfield. My Coach, mentor and friend.

Brian Chernett. Who gave me an opportunity when he didn't know if I could make an IMPACT with Chief Executives.

Mastermind Groups. Roy, Graham and Robin – my original Mastermind Team; thank you for pushing me to become one of Europe's leading speakers. To my current team: Shay, Steff and Steve; thanks for a world of inspiration.

Joanne Bloomfield. A lady with so many talents who has supported me through this whole project. Her dedication and commitment embodies the whole concept of this book, especially when I have not been 'in the room' at many of our meetings. She is a consummate professional who has never quivered in the challenges of writing this book with me.

Steff. My conscience.

John Moseley. For bringing this book to life.

Ali. Someone had to have the job of looking after me. Nobody else in the world puts in as much effort to make sure I'm equipped to IMPACT the world.

Foreword

I am delighted to recommend this book. To all those who wish to be motivated to change or 'continually improve', this is the place to start. I have heard Nigel speak and seen Nigel make an IMPACT on Academy members many times through the years – his power to transform individuals and entire organizations is breathtaking.

His IMPACT presentation has been embraced by tens of thousands of people already and now this book will help hundreds of thousands more pick up on the simple, but devastating, power of creating IMPACT. This simple philosophy is creating positive change all around the world and anyone who takes the leap of faith needed to make their life 'worth living' will be forever in Nigel's debt. In

my opinion, life is definitely worth a little more effort
and with Nigel's support you can make a real difference
in your life – right now, this minute, today.

A best-seller in the making.

Brian Chernett, Founder and CEO of the Academy for
Chief Executives Ltd

Introduction

You've picked up this book. Well done.

But, are you going to do what you always do?

Which is absolutely nothing.

Or

Are you going to give yourself the chance to get the life you deserve?

The choice is yours.

It always has been.

Whether you purchased this book yourself, or you were given it as a gift, the fact that you have this book in your hands means you are probably looking for more from life. Some say they want to be 'happy', others say 'I just want to achieve more'.

Everyone is different – or so it would seem. In fact, we are looking for the same thing: more. We just want it all in different proportions, colours, frequency and intensity.

The good news is getting more is simple. The bad news is that it's going to be one of the most difficult journeys you will ever undertake. I have worked with literally thousands of people over the years, each struggling with their lives to one degree or another. One thing that everyone shares in common is the emotional equivalent of a 'stubborn gravy stain' in their life – the spot they just can't put right no matter what they do. It is entirely possible to excel in virtually every aspect of your day-to-day life, but struggle to make any headway in the one area that is important to get right.

I have learned that in order to get more we have to follow a certain, clearly defined path and stick to it. After years of working with clients I have developed a simple process that literally anyone can follow; I call it The IMPACT Code. It's so straightforward, it's almost laughable, but it takes iron determination to make your life different and the simplicity of my model belies the fundamental nature of its mission – creating IMPACT, achieving more and ultimately getting the life you deserve.

My life has not always run smoothly, in fact there have been times when I have veered so far from my comfort zone I wondered if I would ever get back. With intense highs in my early career and devastating lows (of every kind) that followed in quick succession, I could never describe my life as ideal, but I have a great life and I'm very proud of it – warts and all.

I have been steadfast in my quest to get the best from every experience and ensure that I live the life I want, the life I deserve – even when the most obvious thing to do was give up in the face of my own mistakes. Bottom line: I don't always get it right; neither will you. The important thing to remember is not to give up, but keep going. Remember the six key principles of the model and work on your life the way you work on any important project.

I want to help you achieve at least the level of success that I have enjoyed – which is substantial – and know what it feels like to be truly happy. I want you to love your life as much as I love mine.

So, why bother? Why is creating IMPACT in your life worth the journey? Like you, I have purchased dozens of 'self-help' books from a whole host of modern-day gurus, each promising their own brand of utopia. Unlike you (I'm guessing here), I read them cover to cover before I put them on my bookshelf. It's my job to read them, but I still find it a bit of a chore. You are not alone if you have found it tough to get through some of these books or to find meaning in all that 'chat'. Unfortunately, self-help books are only as good as you are prepared to be; nothing or nobody can help you unless you want to help yourself.

So, we'll assume you want more from life and that you accept that creating IMPACT may be a path that could lead you to the Promised Land. Now is the time to open your mind to a new way of thinking. If you aren't prepared to do that, then put this book down and come back to it when you have tried all of the other techniques and still don't get what you want. This book isn't an instant cure for a dysfunctional life. YOU are the only cure you need for your life.

So, what is stopping you creating IMPACT or allowing positive momentum to start?

Well, for most of us, and especially you, the answer is…

YOU'RE LAZY.

'That's not very nice,' you might say. 'That's not very impactful.'

Well, let's face it, whatever you have read or listened to previously hasn't worked. Otherwise, why are you still looking? Some areas of your life must still need attention or why even get this far into the introduction?

Together we are going to do, think, and create more IMPACT in your life. It is going to be demanding, difficult and at times unpleasant; if that doesn't sit well with you, tough. If you are looking for a quick fix, there isn't one. So, stop wishing and start working. At times it might all seem 'a bit too much like hard work' and that's because it is.

The end result will be worth the investment of your time and energy. If you don't believe me then carefully read the case studies I have included throughout the book and see how ordinary people have changed their lives for the better (often in the face of tremendous adversity) and in doing so have generated tremendous success and have had an enormous IMPACT on the world around them. Incidentally, there is a cash prize for anyone who can find an exceptional person who hasn't worked hard, toiled at their 'art' or shed more than a few gritty tears along the way. The only place you will find 'success' before 'work' is in the dictionary!

It is going to be tough and even though the change may be easy to understand it isn't necessarily going to be easy to do. Anything different, difficult, or challenging will always seem like hard work. If you feel like giving up and going back to familiar territory, consider the fact that your past actions have created your life today; a life you are not entirely satisfied with.

The Code that is locked within the pages of this book is waiting to be cracked and the rewards are more incredible than you could ever imagine. The IMPACT Code will teach you perseverance, tenacity, and most of all, commitment.

A friend of mine once said, 'When all is said and done, much more is said than done.'

I have spent the last seven years working with thousands of people all over the world. From America to Nigeria, Dubai to the Ukraine, from Hungary to Israel and back again, and the one thing I have learned is that we all have the same issues.

Ninety per cent of people I meet and coach want to be loved, appreciated and acknowledged; money is usually far down the list. In fact, most people who seek executive coaching have got the money aspect of their life under control; it's just the rest of their life that sucks. People all around the world are champion blamers – it never ceases to amaze me just what kind of grand delusions people have about the reasons for their unhappiness.

I ask them to categorize what could be done to help get what they want. Most people then launch into a rambling dialogue about what others could do to make their life 'worth living'. So, whenever I ask, 'Are you doing this to or for other people?' I get a look of 'Why should I?' Gandhi said, 'Be the change you want to create.'

Virginia Satir said, 'We all have four basic needs: to be attended to, listened to, touched and mutually respected.' How can we achieve this? Just reading this book isn't enough, though that doesn't mean it won't have a profound IMPACT on you; awareness is the first step to achieving real change. However, we know from research that we – deeply flawed human beings – only remember 25% of what we hear, 50% of what we see and read (i.e., this book) and 75% of what we do. But we retain an amazing 90% if we do and at the same time teach others. So please, don't keep these ideas a secret, do what the book suggests: learn and pass it on, so other people say 'What happened to you?' You don't need to be evangelical on my behalf; I know the IMPACT Code works from the many thousands of testimonials I have received and, most importantly, because my life is so damn good (even the crappy bits take me somewhere better). Share for your own sake. Live the life you want; share it with others and reinforce your behaviour over and over again. Help others. Help yourself.

As I said, reading about IMPACT won't create change, won't give you more of anything of particular note. You MUST implement the Code as soon as possible. Why? It is a fact of human psychology that if we don't start to implement something new within 48 hours of first learning about it, we never will. Surely not? Surely we can take this weekend to indulge in a few last days of comfy, dysfunctional living? No. If it's time to change your life, it's time to do it NOW. Otherwise, suffer the consequences of the Law of Diminishing Effect. If you don't believe me, think back to courses and training you have completed in the past. No doubt you wrote hundreds of notes, decided – categorically – during the long training day to make every minute count, only to file your notes away in your desk drawer on your return, never to look at them again. That, my friend, is called Shelf Development. What we're after here is a good old-fashioned dose of Self Development.

Before we start into the programme it's important to remember that what you will read is my truth; it's not *the*

truth. Whenever you like an idea, implement it immediately, but check…does it feel right? If not (and there's
only a small chance you won't like something), as Joe
Calloway always says – let it go.

However, before you cast an idea into the abyss, you may
want to first consider why it bothers you. Remember, you
are where you are now based on past decisions and actions. Are you tossing the plan because it puts you outside
your comfort zone or because you genuinely don't agree
with it? If you are scared of discomfort then I have only
one thing to say to you: GET OVER IT!

Recognize that you have made choices along the way, and
that's why your life works or stinks. Einstein said, 'The
level of thinking that got you here won't get you to the
new place you want to be.' Smart guy that Einstein fella.

In short, it means you are going to have to DO something different in order to get the result you desire.

Along the way, you will see quotes that I love. Print them
out, place them where you can see them – learn from
them. Again, human behavioural research has observed

that unless we read/listen to something more than five times, it is unlikely to become a habit. Yes. You might have to read this book more than once. No apologies.

The whole memory-effect phenomenon is everywhere to be seen. That's why your kids seem to remember every single word of their favourite pop songs; if it were you or me, we would listen once and hope to memorize the words. You have to believe in the reality of what we are – inherently lazy creatures. Fight the urge to be lazy and stick with the programme. I have lots of strategies for remembering good lessons or learning from experiences. You can develop your own, but some of the tricks that work best for me are making notes in books, using a highlighter pen to mark key passages, and reading everything that resonates with me several times (I have got books I have read literally dozens of times). Instead of lending your favourite books out, buy your friends their own copy. At the back of the book I have recommended several great books – get on with reading, make learning your priority. Make positive change your mission.

Most people – and I assume by buying this book you are not one of them – say they want a better life but are not

prepared to put in the work necessary to get the job done.
Notice I didn't say hard work. The tasks themselves are
not hard, but the change can be very uncomfortable at
times, making it 'feel' hard. Ed Foreman, the only sena-
tor to win two different Senates in United States' history,
said, 'Winners are those people who constantly do the
things that losers find uncomfortable.'

All change, at first, feels uncomfortable. Accept that and
you are well on your way to success. My job is to teach
you how to be comfortable just 'being' – during change,
periods of status quo and even the odd backward step.

Do you remember driving a car for the first time? Going
out on your first date with your first love? What about
the first time you rode a bike without stabilizers? At first
you stumbled, were completely awkward, scared and
you probably screwed it all up. Can you imagine a child
taking the same attitude to walking as we adults take to
living? If a baby gave up at the first fall, or decided, 'forget
this, I could get hurt,' we would all be shuffling along on
our bottoms. Apart from the fact that it would be hell on

your clothes and would cost a fortune in cleaning bills, what would life be like if we had given up on walking! We grow up to be lazy; we start out as champions.

Making change in your life ultimately means making IM-PACT in other people's lives. Some people are so beaten up they believe they aren't capable of making even the smallest bit of IMPACT. Not true. Absolutely not true.

As Dame Anita Roddick once said, 'If you think you are too small to make any impact, try going to bed with a mosquito in the room.'

So, are you ready to start or do you want to continue bitching about how life is not giving you what you deserve? It's entirely up to you. If you want more, accept responsibility for your own life and behaviour; stop whining and start working.

I challenge you to get more IMPACT in your life. I hope you can love yourself enough to do what is best for you.

Never compromise on what makes you happy. Life is very short. Let me help you make it sweeter.

> 'It's never too late to be the person you could have been.'
>
> – *George Eliot*

With all my heart I wish you success.

– Nigel Risner

How to use this book

Are you in a hurry? Sitting on a plane or train or waiting for the kids to come home from school? You're probably just impatient to unlock the riddle of the IMPACT Code. So, let me help you. I have designed this book for a bit of speed reading followed by a lot of careful consideration and soul searching. If you want to get a quick feel of the IMPACT Code then you will see that each section is structured in the same way:

- The big idea
- A summary of that element of the Code
- Detail about how to implement the Code

- An exercise to help you implement the Code.

Every other page has a quote attached to it – not necessarily relevant to the section, but as you read the book over again you will start to find quotes that mean something to you. Copy them out, carry them with you in your head and, more importantly, in your heart.

What's the big idea?

I said the code was simple and I wasn't joking. Each letter of the word IMPACT represents something important; a powerful but simple message. I have highlighted what the 'big idea' for each section is and then followed it with a summary of how that element of the code works and what it hopes to achieve. That said, you have to read the detail to make it work, but I am a firm believer that there really isn't any time quite like the present. You don't have to know the detail to start thinking about the concepts immediately. You will be amazed what comes to mind even after the first read. As long as you are honest with yourself (and that is not as easy to be as it sounds) then you will start to open your mind and your heart to a new way of thinking and being.

Read this book at least twice; your first read could be clouded by your own desire to prove any new theory wrong. Our inner demons will do all they can to keep us attached to what makes us comfortable. All I am saying is that your initial reaction might not be based on whether you think I am talking garbage, but in fact on your inner fear of change.

If you read it twice and you like it, keep it. Don't give it to a friend. Buy them a copy (you really will be helping me with that one!) and use yours as a reference point. You will get things wrong and you will forget what it's all about. You will. Get your marker pen out and start high-lighting what you want to remember in the book – write all over it if you have to. Buy a lovely notepad or journal and map your progress. Clip articles that inspire you and put them in the journal. Write down everything that makes you proud or make a note when you do something you didn't think you could. Make notes, draw doodles. In short, start to document your change. When you are feel-ing down nothing will lift you up faster than your 'success journal'.

Dig in.

CHAPTER ONE

The Impact Code

I = In the room

If you're in the room, be in the room

In the room – summary

'The past is a place of reference, not a place of residency.' – *Willie Jollie.*

The only place you can be is here; make the most of it, don't waste the opportunity to make the best of it.

Focus.

In order to create the future, you need to forgive the past.

Acknowledge success, recognize your own strengths.

Visualize success, imagine how it will feel, practice remembering positive experiences.

Daydream.

If you're in the room,
be in the room

I know what you're thinking.

'That's the silliest thing I have ever heard. If I am in the room, I'm already there…idiot!'

You'd think so wouldn't you? It makes sense, after all, where else could you be but in the same place as the one you are standing in? If only it were that simple.

In all aspects of your life if you are not 'in the room', you are not in the game. Period. By that I don't mean physically, I mean mentally in the room; right where you are supposed to be. In short, you have to be exactly where you need to be – you need to focus on that moment or opportunity to make it count and block out everything else.

'That's easy,' you say, 'if all I have to do to get more from my life is concentrate during meetings, then this is going to be a piece of cake!'

Good luck with that. Nothing is ever as straightforward as it seems. Here is a little puzzle. What do you see when you look at the following sentence:

OPPORTUNITYISNOWHERE

Well? What have you got?

Opportunity is nowhere?
Opportunity is snow here?
Opportunity is now here?

If you are lucky and you read it as it was intended, you would have seen 'opportunity is now here'. But if you are like the vast majority of adults you probably read 'opportunity is nowhere'. What's my point? Simple,

Never have regrets, follow your heart. – *Hillary Richards*

really. Given the subject matter of this book, had you stopped and read it carefully you would have made the proper deduction. If you did, then good for you. But pretty much all of us are not where we should be when it counts and so we probably read it with 'negative' eyes. Why do we do it? Why don't we concentrate on the moment and make the most of every opportunity? Because we are human, that's why.

We are all either permanent inhabitants of the past or we worry WAY too much about the future and what MIGHT happen. It is absolutely mind-blowing how much baggage we all carry around with us and nothing is more likely to get in the way of your success then your own personal truckload of it.

Do you ever talk to yourself? You probably just did. I think we all do to a certain extent, but each and every one of us has a permanent internal dialogue raging on, controlling virtually everything we do. Our past experiences gradually become a voice in our head and unless we train ourselves to hear a different voice, it will work its evil and affect our behaviour in a way that won't necessarily help us move forward. We make choices based on what we have experienced and that seriously affects how we perceive the world. Naturally, experience shapes behaviour and thank heavens for maturity, but there are actually three voices battling it out inside your head: the Commentator, the Coach and the Player. Your goal is to become a successful Player and in order to do that you have to learn how to listen all over again.

Like any sports commentator, your internal Commentator can only comment on what has happened – it's a historian. Commentators don't carry a game forward. That voice is your past. 'Don't do that, you might fail and everyone will laugh at you!'; 'Don't talk to him; you don't know him; what if he doesn't like you?' No matter how big and bad we get, we are all just big kids inside; frightened of rejection, failure and pain. The internal Commentator plays right into that fear and keeps us back,

There's always one moment in life when the door opens and lets the future in. – *Graham Greene*

keeps us out of the room and more to the point, right in the middle of our 'comfort zone'.

On the other hand, there is the Coach. Any Coach takes your past experience and channels it into a game plan, a fearless strategy in the face of possible failure, a way to achieve your dreams and goals. The Coach will take you outside of your comfort zone, but he will arm you with valuable advice, support and guidance.

The Coach in your head would say, 'Have a go at that, you've done it before and it didn't work out but you learned from that. Nobody is going to laugh at you.' Or he would say. 'Go and talk to him, you don't know him but he probably doesn't know anyone here either – you never know, he might hold the key to a brilliant new opportunity. He will like you. You are a nice person.'

Do you see where I am going with this? When you are in the middle of a situation are you really there (being a Player) or are you cowering behind the past or rigid with fear about the future? We have to learn to ignore the negativity that spouts forth from the Commentator and start developing the Coach within us. The Commentator comes from the past – he has important lessons to look back on, but he can't help you move forward. The Coach puts you 'in the room', the Commentator keeps you at the door and out of harm's way.

The game of life is merciless with its team selection. It has chosen you to play out your life and there aren't any substitutes to fall back on if the going gets rough. Consider where you spend most of your time; past, present or future? Every good Player needs a Coach to keep moving ahead of the game, but he knows that winning means staying in the game. So, think about how you can make more IMPACT as a player who listens to his coach.

This point was painfully demonstrated in the infamous European Cup Final match in 1999 between Bayern Munich and Manchester United. After 89 minutes of a 90-minute game, Bayern Munich was one goal up and from the look on their faces and that of the players on the bench, they were already celebrating in readiness

Be faithful to that which exists nowhere but in yourself.
– *André Gide*

of the final whistle. One of Manchester United's key strengths is that they never give up and they always play until they hear the final whistle. And even with only 40 seconds to play they were giving it everything they had. Just seconds before the match moved into injury time, Manchester United equalized. Play continued for another two minutes, but the Bayern Munich players, managers and substitutes were unprepared for the sudden turn of events and seemed to pay no attention to the rest of the match. Manchester United, on the other hand, had even more energy than before and thought, 'Let's go for it!' A minute later they scored. Even more remarkable than the last-minute goal was the fact that several of the Bayern Munich players thought it was all over two minutes before the end; they could have kept fighting for the chance to win on penalties but they didn't.

The referee had to literally pick up one of the players off the field and tell him to continue playing. Thank goodness Manchester United did not do the same thing when they were one-nil down. What were the Bayern players thinking? 'Oh, we've done enough now, we've never lost in the last minute of a game.' Every member of that team had stopped listening to their Coach and turned up the volume of their Commentator. The Coach would have told them, 'Watch out, Manchester United is a formidable team, they are hungry for success and never waste a minute – keep fighting to the end, you can still win if you try and if you don't, you gave it your best shot.'

There are so many lessons to be learned from this one football match and I suppose the question is, if it is your dream and your passion is there ever a time to quit? I know what my answer is – what is yours? What baffles me about the Bayern players and people in general is why wouldn't you give it everything you've got? What were they saving it for? What are you saving yourself for?

Experience can only help us when we put it where it belongs – in the past. After all, we know that the past is a place of reference not a place of residency! The most important thing to always remember is this: when you are in the middle of a situation forget about the future. The only place you can be is here and now and you have to make the most of every minute of every day.

Put your future in good hands – your own.
– *Mark Victor Hanson*

The past

There's more to it then simply switching off a negative voice in our head. The past is who we are, but it doesn't add up to what we can be. You can't change the past, so park it. Acknowledge disaster, cruelty, bitterness and grief. Understand how the sum of your experiences really affects you today. We all roll our eyes at the thought of counsellors and psychiatrists unravelling our childhood and blaming our parents for all of our adult woes. I know I've done it myself, but what we all fail to see is that they have a valid point. In fact, all they are doing is trying to oust some very destructive demons and help people build a more positive future. It sounds clichéd and I guess maybe it is, but that is because it is true for each and every one of us. Things only become clichéd when they are so common that they no longer surprise us; it doesn't make them any less relevant.

None of us can escape our past, but we all have a chance to make a better future. In order to move forward we must learn to forgive the past. Start with the people who have hurt you in some way, then learn to forgive yourself. Whatever role you played in your past you must forgive yourself. Open your heart to forgiveness and be amazed at the sense of calm that will flow through you. You might think that some people cannot be forgiven for their sins against you – particularly if you have been abused – but forgiveness is your first step to regaining control of your life and holding on to your power. Forgive them all. Forgive yourself.

'Forgive us our trespasses, as we forgive those who trespass against us.'
                                    The Lord's Prayer, The Christian Bible

As a personal and professional Coach, I hear so many heartbreaking stories. Good, solid people who have gone on to have great success, but remain crippled by their past. The past just keeps holding them back, keeping them inside the box of 'the known'. It's painful to see how

How we spend our days, is of course how we spend our lives.
– *Annie Dillard*

many people sabotage their own success simply because
they are frightened to try something new or acknowledge
the real issues that haunt their daily lives.

I'm not suggesting that everyone should rush out and sign
up for thousands of pounds' worth of therapy (that said,
you would be surprised how helpful professional counselling can be). No, the first step to getting more from
your future is to simply acknowledge your past. Break it
down into key areas of development (write it down if you
have to). Get inside the real issues and see how they make
you feel today. Were you laughed at by your family as a
kid for having 'wacky' ideas? Does that hold you back at
work today because you don't like to be creative 'out in
the open'? Did one of your trusted relatives abuse you?
Do you wear a mask to hide the real you, the one that is
actually still frightened of giving away your power and
of being hurt again? Did you never feel good enough to
earn your parents' respect? Do you overcompensate for
everything – trying so hard nobody can keep up? The list
goes on.

You have to remember that your parents and all of the people you meet in your day-to-day life are just as messed up as you are. Now there's a thought! No wonder our parents made mistakes – maybe they were doing the best they could in the circumstances and given their own personal baggage. Remember, when our parents were struggling to raise us they didn't have the help we have today. Self-help books, counsellors, family support groups, etc. did not exist back then. With the exception of Dr Spock, they didn't have anywhere to turn for advice…other than their parents! I know that it's no excuse for bad behaviour, but you have to move on, no matter how bad your experiences have been. If you can't do it alone, get help, but get this job done.

When you think about it, our parents never stood a chance of getting it right. Neither do you. You will make mistakes, but from now on you have to learn good lessons from them and stop the Commentator getting in the way of success.

We all say we want success, but that in itself can be scary. More people than you care to imagine are as frightened

Listen to your dreams – those are the sounds
no one else can hear. – *Kobi Yamada*

of success as they are of failure. I don't mean they cower
behind a chair crying, 'Oh nooooo, not another promo-
tion, get it away from me!' In fact, most people simply
avoid success. We all of us have the means of realizing our
dreams, but if we actually had our dream come true what
would it be like? Would it be as good as we dreamed?
Would we be bitterly disappointed? What if it was short-
lived; how we would we cope with losing it all? What if
people got jealous and didn't like us any more? Oh yes, we
have all thought these thoughts at one time or another.
Success can be just as much of a challenge as failure – very
often we just opt out of success to avoid the possibility of
change and fear of taking a risk. We sabotage our future
to stay nearer to our past; nearer to our comfort zone.

Change of any kind is scary, but if you want more out of
life you are going to have to learn how to cope outside of
your personal safety zone. The easiest way to step forward
and leave the past behind is to 'be in the room'.

When you quiet the voice of your Commentator and
learn to listen to your Coach you will quickly see how
easy it is to let go of the past. When you are in a meeting, concentrate all of your energy on that meeting, don't

drift off and don't start second-guessing yourself based on something your mother said to you when you were five! If you make a mistake, so what? If you are helping your son to do his homework, be where he needs you to be, by his side, not back in the office. When you focus your energy on the present the future will start taking care of itself. Yes we need a plan, but your only job today is to fulfil just one part of that plan, not solve the whole puzzle. One step at a time, one day at a time.

You can never hope to create IMPACT and reap the benefits of its ripple effect unless you start to live and think differently. Small people can make a huge difference to the whole world – ask anyone who worked with Mother Teresa or Gandhi. You don't have to be loud to make an IMPACT. But you do have to be present.

People often mistake being 'in the room' as a call to make a dramatic impression on everyone there. You don't have to participate to be present and you don't have to make a tangible IMPACT with every step you take to make an IMPACT in the lives of those around you and ultimately

You are the one who can stretch your own horizon.
– *Edgar Magnin*

in your own life. I'll say it again, just in case you missed it the first time. You have to be present.

Ian Woosnam was playing golf in the British Open and at the end of the penultimate round he was in second place. On the last day, he opened up with a fantastic birdie that put him firmly in the lead, but just as he was about to play his second hole his caddie, Miles Byrne, informed him that by mistake he had not counted the clubs in his bag and he noticed he had too many clubs. This would cost him two shots; nothing to really worry about but he did what most of us do when we allow negative detail to cloud our minds, we focus on what should have been and not what is. For the next five holes his mind was anywhere but on the game in hand; he was more than likely raging about his caddie and not concentrating on what he had to do to win. He stopped focusing on winning and started concentrating on not losing. Ian Woosnam said his caddy cost him £230,000. Who do you think cost him the money? I know my money isn't on the caddy. Remember when you are on the golf course – BE THERE.

If you are in the room, BE in the room.

Here are a few quick lessons that will help you get started with being in the room – things everyone should know about life.

- 99% of people are nice, don't be afraid to give them a chance.
- People want to help you succeed.
- Nobody laughs at you for trying.
- There is no such thing as failure, there are only results.
- You don't have to suffer bad people or bad situations, you have the power.
- Your life is yours alone. Nobody can live it for you.
- If you live your life with a whole heart you will never regret anything.

The serious point is that when you start being honest with yourself you can start to understand what it is from your past that haunts you today. Fear of rejection? Fear of failure? Fear of betrayal? Your problem might be one that needs professional support in order to neutralize it. This is particularly true of sexual and physical abuse. This type of experience has a devastating effect on its victims, but

Difficulties make you a jewel. – *Japanese proverb*

like any other experience it doesn't have to define your life. Get help to put the past where it belongs.

If you don't feel your problem is of that nature, you might still want to talk to a good friend about your feelings. Find someone who loves you enough to tell you the truth – a 'yes' person won't help you get over your past. Sharing an experience and talking about how it affects you today is one of the fastest ways of putting it to rest. Once you start talking, pause for a moment and listen. You will see that virtually everyone has got a story to tell. We are all unique, but we are all human beings at our core; predisposed to hunt, procreate and nurture. As a result we all seem to fall foul of the same types of problems.

What happens when you lose your job? You lose your ability to provide for your family – to hunt. What happens if we fall in love and it falls apart before we have a chance to complete a natural relationship cycle? We lose our chance for procreation and have to start all over again. What happens if we lose a child or any loved one for that matter? We have nurtured and feel lost without that precious life in our lives – we lose our sense of purpose.

Everything that happens to us shapes who we are, but not always for the better. As children we are at the mercy of the adult world and sometimes it lets us down. We want to make things better for our own children but still, we just can't get past what happened to us. Victims of abuse often become overprotective of their children, stifling their every move, which creates as many problems as the abuse caused for the parent in the first place. People who have been betrayed find it impossible to trust anyone and so they don't delegate or open up their hearts to another person. They become lonely and often very bitter and their life stalls. The results of living in the past are dramatic and rarely positive.

Getting the life you deserve means that must learn to let go of the past, once and for all. You have to learn to live with yourself so you can start living for yourself.

It gets dark sometimes, but morning comes. Keep hope alive.
– *Jesse Jackson*

You need to develop the voice of your Coach. Consider experiences you have had in the past and ask yourself why you didn't give it your best shot. Ask why you crave approval. Why do you need the love of another person to feel valuable? Why do you need to succeed at the expense of every other aspect of your life? I've said it before; I'll no doubt be saying it again. Because we are human – flawed, beautiful creatures whose complexities are as many and varied as the days are long – we are all alike. We all get scared about the future, about failure, about loss. Lurking in every closet is an Encyclopedia Britannica of personal issues that needs to be filed under the section 'been there, done that, moving on now, thank you.'

> 'The past is a place of reference, not a place of residency.'
>
> *– Willie Jollie*

> 'The saddest words of tongue or pen are these four words – it might have been.'
>
> *– Oliver Wendell Holmes*

Anyway

People are often unreasonable, illogical,
And self-centered
Forgive them anyway.

If you are kind, people may accuse you
Of selfish, ulterior motives;
Be kind anyway.

If you are successful, you will win some
False friends and some true enemies;
Succeed anyway.

If you are honest and frank,
People may cheat you;
Be honest and frank anyway.

What you spend years building, someone
Could destroy overnight;
Build anyway.

Either we have our dreams or we live our dreams.
– *Zoe Koplowitz*

If you find serenity and happiness,
They may be jealous;
Be happy anyway.

The good you do today,
People will often forget tomorrow;
Do good anyway.

Give the world the best you have,
And it may never be enough;
Give the world the best you've got anyway.

You see, in the final analysis,
It is between you and God;
It was never between you and them anyway.

— Anonymous, found on the wall
of Mother Teresa's office

Take the good things from the past

Yes, there is good stuff in the past too; it isn't all doom and gloom. What we need to carry forward is success and positive learning. The question is how to bring positive experiences forward without getting bogged down in all the negative stuff.

It is far too easy to overlook our own successes. One of the exercises I challenge my clients with is to quickly write down ten personal successes they can remember. Try and do that yourself, right now.

It is surprisingly difficult to do, isn't it? Part of the problem is that difficult situations or things that hurt our feelings seem to leave a much deeper impression on our

Start a crusade in your life – to dare to be your best.
– *William Danforth*

consciousness than good experiences. Who knows why we do it, but we all suffer from a lack of positive memory recall. If you close your eyes and really think about it you probably can start to remember a whole host of successes, but the fact that you have to try is testimony to the way we are as human beings.

To get to grips with why we keep delving into the scary stuff when faced with a new situation, we need to take a quick look at how the brain works.

What is the brain?

The human brain weighs in at about 1450 g and looks like a squishy blanched walnut. It is deliciously complex and yet is made up only three key systems which have evolved with us over the millennia. What is utterly fascinating is that from cave man to space man, our brains have been constantly evolving; who knows what we will be capable of in another 50,000 years?

Our spinal cord and the brain stem are the oldest part of our brain (proto-reptilian brain) and takes care of basic physiological needs such as eating, moving, breathing and sleeping. It keeps the body in constant balance and when it registers an imbalance it sends out a signal to correct it. For example, when you have drunk too much water and you need to go to the toilet, you 'feel' it. It is also said that the brainstem is the home of our instincts. Nobody really knows the true nature of instincts. The problem is that nothing we 'learn' affects them (which means scientists

There is nothing we cannot live down,
rise above or overcome. – *Ella Wheeler-Wilcox*

can't get a handle on it because they can't affect them in any way). The reality is that we have virtually no control over our instincts which makes us all deliciously emotional beings.

The second brain system is called the 'old cortex' and contains the forehead and limbic systems. This is our emotional powerhouse and it is where we store both our feelings and expressive reactions. The old cortex is very sensitive to images and analogue (non-verbal) communication. Images conjure up powerful emotions which in turn determine behaviour.

Third, and by no means least (it is in fact the largest part of the brain), is the neocortex or more commonly known as the cerebral cortex. We got this baby about 50,000 years ago and it is where our higher brain functions reside. It is huge, but is folded and layered in such a way as to fit inside our skull. Here we find speaking, language, thinking, ethics, morals and just about any other human capacity you can think of. However, a large chunk of this area of the brain has no clearly-defined function and scientists believe that it is here that we process and store information.

You may have heard about the differences between the left and right side of the brain already, but just to clarify here is a brief outline of what happens in each area. The left half of the brain is geared towards logic and prefers detail. This is the part of your brain that is constantly analysing the meaning of perceptions and looking for facts and figures. But it can't work its magic and help us live out our day-to-day lives without the help of the right side of the brain.

The right half of the brain looks at the 'big picture' and searches for coherence in all that information. The logical left wants to reveal an exact meaning, whereas the right is more focused on the point of it all. The right is centred on emotional stimuli, relationships and other less tangible realities. The two halves of the brain are connected by a thick fibre called the corpus callosum: your own personal information super-highway. Together they enable

Sticking to it is the genius. – *Thomas Edison*

us to reason our way through the day but what is clear is
that emotion rules the roost.

Memory is formed as a part of a hugely complex process
of synaptic activity that creates neural networks or paths.
Nobody really knows how this works and for now we will
just accept that this process is constantly occurring. Every
time we experience something it triggers a million different reactions inside our brain which eventually lead to the
formation of memory – an engram.

The hippocampus is where we store short-term memory
and surprisingly accounts for just three per cent of our brain
tissue. It is here that recent experiences are sent for processing. The hippocampus then flashes messages back to the
cortex and so the more we experience the same the thing,
the more deeply embedded the memory becomes. Eventually the hippocampus does not need to recall them to affect
behaviour. Thus our experiences become embedded in
long term memory and go on to affect our behaviour at an
almost 'instinctive' level.

The hippocampus is pretty selective about which memories it sends to long-term storage (otherwise our heads would explode by the time we are two years old). So, now you start to see how the more impactful an experience is, or the more often it occurs, the more likely it is to be buried deep inside your noggin. Now you can understand why stuff that your parents did – which by the very nature of parenting means that they did it over and over again – has such a pronounced effect on you as you grow older.

In addition, we cannot escape our evolution, and the oldest part of our brain functions to protect us. Our instinct is to 'RUN AS FAST AS YOU CAN!' at the first sign of danger. Now you can see why functioning outside of your comfort zone is so difficult. Your brain doesn't want you to hurt or be in danger and so it tries to cajole you into playing it safe.

The bottom line is that bad stuff usually makes a deeper impression on us than good stuff and we have to train

Not all birds can fly. What separates the flyers from the walkers is the ability to take off. – *Carl Sagan*

ourselves to recall the good stuff. We have to artificially
remind ourselves how great we are to make sure that we
build a neural defence system to combat our own fears.
Over time, and with practice, things that bother you
won't because the logical part of your brain will learn a
new logic. It's OK to try; it's OK to take that kind of risk
because I am not in any mortal danger and I will still
be able to eat, sleep, pee and procreate when I am done.
Thus, working outside of the zone and inside the room
will get easier and easier.

If you doubt the theory, think back to when you were
first learning to ride a bike or when you were teaching
your kid to do it. When a kid first gets on a bike without
stabilizers they have no balance and it seems impossibly
hard to do. The first time we try anything the hippocampus is processing the information, dealing with balance
and trying to rationalize what we are trying to do. It's
tough as it has no frame of reference. So we get it wrong
more than we get it right.

Remember what it felt like, constantly falling off? Sometimes you would get a bit further along, but eventually you would fall off again. Then, suddenly in the briefest second, it all clicks into place and you, or your kid, can ride a bike. You never fall off again. The feeling is incredible. In fact, your hippocampus has been constantly sending multiple messages back to the cortex and when it is has stored enough information to make an indelible memory, it is 'filed' in such a way that you no longer have to consciously 'recall' it to be able to do it. Thus you become instantly able to complete the task on what feels like an instinctive level. From car wreck to world-champion cyclist in a less than a heart beat.

Each of us has a spark of life inside us, and our highest
endeavour ought to be to set off that spark in one another.
– *Kenny Ausubel*

The engram square dance

It's time to dust off your mental shoes and make some room in that tired old brain for the finer things in life. Practice really does make perfect in this case. The more you force yourself to acknowledge success and what makes you a great person, the more likely it is that the volume control on your Coach will start to move upwards. Think of it as emotional line dancing. You are going to allow yourself to remember all the great things you do so that eventually the steps to this dance become second nature. In time, those good ol' boys in the left side of your brain will start dancing in step with those free wheeling gals on the right. Easy!

At the core of the IMPACT Code is action, but we'll cover that in detail later. I've already mentioned that people remember a staggering 90% of the information they process if they do and teach at the same time. Now you know why. The physical act of doing something positive and the emotional benefit of teaching it to another person will start to form very stable neural networks in your brain. Gandhi got it right when he said, 'Be the change you want to create'.

I am a big exponent of writing things down, keeping notes, taking pictures of happy memories with you where ever you go. We all – even me – need them. I still get scared about taking risks and trying new things, but I understand why and I have developed a coping strategy that helps me get past the fear. One of my most important tools is my Success Journal. I have dozens of them now, but I always carry one with me where ever I go, just in case I fall foul of the Commentator (who occupies a very large house in the left side of my brain). I write all sorts of stuff down in it. Every day I manage to do something that I consider a success. Sometimes just getting through my workload and being home in time for dinner is a feat that seems to defy the laws of physics. I write it down; it reminds me that I can.

Follow your heart even when others scoff. Don't be beaten
down by naysayers. – *Howard Schultz*

I have pictures of my kids, my wife and me on holiday, testimonials from happy customers, thank-you letters, and notes about successful pitches – all kinds of stuff. This portable book of 'goodness' inspires me, comforts me and teaches me that there is so much success in my life and that without change I wouldn't have half of it. Let me tell you, I never have trouble recalling ten successes. My problem is limiting my answer to just ten.

One of the most insightful comments I have ever heard, and one I repeat to people over and over, was made by Dr Phil McGraw when he said, 'we teach people how to treat us' and that applies to every aspect of our life. You cannot achieve IMPACT without creating success for others. Learning to live with yourself will also help you live with others. Be kind, be generous (and I don't mean with your cash). It feels great and in time it creates a positive shift in the world that surrounds you. Good things really do come to good people.

Anther important technique for 'reprogramming' our brains into believing we 'can' is to dream about it. Visualize the success you want, take time over your dream, and imagine what it will feel like to get what your heart desires. Repeat this visualization process every day. Take quiet time each day to think about nothing else but what you want from life. Go wild, enjoy it.

Remember, the more you feel it, the more likely you are to believe that you can achieve it. Daydreaming is not just for kids and actors! Dreaming is vital for everyone as it helps us develop creativity. Too many people fall victim to the thought that as you get older you have to stop dreaming about what life might be. Rubbish. Dreaming is for grown-ups too.

Make daydreaming (or meditating if you want to get spiritual about it) part of your daily routine. But I urge you to develop a fixed picture of what you want and practice imagining how it will feel and keep going to that

Dreams don't die until we let them. – *James Ojala*

'place' as often as possible (especially if you are feeling nervous about change or making the necessary changes to realize that dream). This, combined with positive action and frequent use of your success journal, will significantly improve the effectiveness of the IMPACT Code and is the key to unlocking your potential.

You can also link this visualization process into your success journal. A good friend of mine, Reg Athwal (an excellent speaker on the subject of hiring staff), has created a 'Future Photo Album'. He has pictures and images of things he dreams about and it's not just about possessions, it could be of kids, an attractive partner, or anything else that takes your fancy. Add these images to your success journal and help support the visualization process.

'What I dream, can happen.'

– Cass Elliante

Small stone, big ripple

If you are obsessing about the scale of change you need to make; then take a step back. I will cover how to achieve your goals in more detail later, but it is important that you fully grasp the concept that change does not have to be big in order to create real and lasting IMPACT. In fact, a tiny shift can make an enormous difference.

Early in my speaking career I was lucky to hear a lecture where this point was made using an extremely vivid example and it really hit a nerve for me. The lecturer started to boil a kettle of water and he informed us that literally seconds before the kettle boiled the temperature of the water was 211 Fahrenheit. Stay with me on this one; like me at this point in the explanation, you are thinking, 'Who cares?' He said that at the moment the water temperature hits 212 degrees Fahrenheit it boils. Big deal?

The bravest sight in the world is someone fighting against the odds. – *Franklin Lane*

But wait a minute and think about that. When water boils it creates steam, which is pretty powerful stuff; after all, it can move trains. Nothing of any consequence happens at 211 Fahrenheit, but with just a one degree shift the potential energy in the water is unleashed. Eureka!

If a one-degree shift can make such a big difference to the water, imagine what you could achieve if you shifted your life up a gear by just one per cent. I am not asking you to shift your thinking by 30 or 40%, but I am asking you to commit to a one per cent shift in everything you do. Not much to ask? Even you can do that?

E+R=0

One of the most important lessons I ever learned I took from a course conducted by my mentor, Jack Canfield. This simple formula helps me focus on what I am doing and why.

E+R=O means that the Events or Experiences in our life plus the Response we give it equal our Outcome.

Right now – and remember that's all there is – how do you feel about your work, your relationships, and your family? You see, in life, how you feel and how you choose to react, is totally up to you.

'Even under the most terrible conditions of psychic and physical stress, we, who lived in concentration camps, can remember men who walked through the huts to comfort others and gave away their last pieces of bread. They may have been few in numbers

We are called upon to become creators, to make the world new. – *John Elof Boodin*

but they offered sufficient proof that everything can
be taken from a man but one thing, the last and the
greatest of human freedoms, to choose one's attitude
in any given set of circumstances, to choose one's
own way of life.'

         – *Victor Frankl,* Man's Search for Meaning

People don't make you feel good or bad – we do that all
by ourselves. Eleanor Roosevelt said, 'No-one can make
us feel inferior without our prior consent.'

So, if you don't like how you are feeling about an
EVENT, change your response and you will see that you
get a different outcome to the one you feared. This will
allow you to be in control of NOW.

E+R=O

You don't need to be a mathematician to work it out. You
control your destiny. Take charge of it and set your future
free.

Set Free

The future is for me.
Nothing can stop it rushing;
one step in the right direction
suddenly the landscape is ahead,
not behind me.

Today there is no more dread.
A sharp wind rushes around me.
Fresh, clean air,
the feelings of darkness and doom
all gone.

Where will I go? What will I do?

Only I can decide.

Only I will decide.

— Joanne Bloomfield

We need to give ourselves permission to act out our dreams
and visions. Even if it takes a lifetime. *— Vijali Hamilton*

Get back in that room!

Starting to drift? Wondering why you started reading this book?

Let me remind you again. The single most important change you can make in terms of creating IMPACT is to GET BACK INTO THE ROOM!

Let's see how you are doing. How about we play a little game? A simple quiz?

Firstly, what did you immediately think when I said 'Let's play a little game'? Was it something like this: 'Oh no, I hate games. What if I get it wrong? What does that say about me if I can't get a simple question right?' Jeez…

So, the Commentator is still shouting loudest then? Your Coach would say, 'Cool, an exciting opportunity to try something new.' The player would say, 'Let's go for it!' So, here's the puzzle:

Connect all of the dots with straight lines without taking
your pen off the paper and going back over the same line
twice.

Complete the nine-dot puzzle with no more than four
lines and the sixteen-dot version with no more than six
straight lines.

You will see that I have given you two since some of you
will already know the first one. Remember, everything is
possible. The answer is at the back of the book. I've given
you the answer, because without it you won't be able to
concentrate (the door will close on every room until you
read the answer at the back…you can't fight nature!).
How did you get on? If you haven't seen it before, and

The tragedy of life is not that it ends soon, but that
we wait so long to begin it. – *W. M. Lewis*

you aren't a mathematical whiz, I bet you are thinking about cheating already.

If you look at the answer before trying to work it out, you shouldn't be surprised if you aren't making enough IMPACT in your life. If you always look for the easy way out, chances are you will find it and you won't like it when you get there. Sometimes you have to work at it. Remember, every time you do the puzzle and you don't succeed, it is a result, not a failure. If you can stay in the room long enough to try you will learn more than you could ever imagine. A right answer isn't necessarily success.

What did you tell yourself? What did you do? What did you achieve?

Think carefully before moving on. Go back and read this section again if you have to. But before you move on, commit to being IN THE ROOM.

Tempus fugit

Each of us is born with a personal bank account. Its name is TIME. Every morning, it credits you with 86,400 seconds. Every night it writes off as lost whatever of this you have failed to invest to good purpose. It carries over no balance. It allows no overdraft. Each day it opens a new account for you. Each night it burns the remains of the day. If you fail to use the day's deposits, the loss is yours. There is no going back. There is no drawing against tomorrow. You must live in the present and focus on today's deposits. Invest your time wisely and you will receive the utmost in health, happiness and success.

The clock is ticking. Try not to waste another second. That doesn't mean filling your every waking moment with a frenetic schedule of tasks; dreaming, relaxing and sleeping are more valuable than virtually all of your other daily tasks. If you feel you have got time to waste, then you are either lying to yourself or you haven't learned to appreciate the real value of life. Make the most of today. Dream, do, live.

In the time of your life – live! – *William Shakespeare*

To realize the value of ONE YEAR, ask a student who failed a grade.

To realize the value of ONE MONTH, ask a mother who gave birth to a premature baby.

To realize the value of ONE WEEK, ask the editor of a weekly newspaper.

To realize the value of ONE HOUR, ask the lovers who are waiting to meet.

To realize the value of ONE MINUTE, ask a person who missed the train.

To realize the value of ONE SECOND, ask a person who just avoided an accident.

To realize the value of ONE MILLISECOND, ask the person who won a silver medal in the Olympics.

Real time IMPACT

'Daddy, may I ask you a question?' asked the little boy.

'Yeah, sure, what is it?' replied the man.

'Daddy, how much money do you make an hour?'

'That's none of your business! What makes you ask such a thing?' the man said angrily.

'I just want to know. Please tell me, how much to do you make an hour?' pleaded the little boy.

'If you must know, I make £20 an hour.'

'Oh,' the little boy replied, head bowed. Looking up he said, 'Daddy, may I borrow £10, please?'

His father was furious. 'If the only reason you wanted to know how much money I make is just so you can bor-

If you love life, do not squander time. That is the stuff
life is made of! – *Ben Franklin*

row some to buy a silly toy or some other nonsense, then you march yourself straight to your room and go to bed. Think about why you're being so selfish. I work long, hard hours every day and don't have time for such child-ish games.'

The little boy quietly went to his room and shut the door. The man sat down and started to get even madder about the little boy's questioning. How dare he ask such ques-tions only to get some money? After an hour or so, the man had calmed down, and started to think he may have been a little hard on his son. Maybe there was something he really needed to buy with that £10 and, besides, he re-ally didn't ask for money very often. The man went to the little boy's room and opened the door.

'Are you asleep, son?' he asked.

'No, Daddy, I'm awake,' replied the boy.

'I've been thinking, maybe I was too hard on you earlier,' said the man. 'It's been a long day and I took my aggravation out on you. Here's the £10 you asked for.'

The little boy sat straight up, beaming. 'Oh, thank you, Daddy!' he yelled. Then, reaching under his pillow, he pulled out some more crumpled up bills. The man, seeing the boy already had money, started to get angry again. The little boy slowly counted his money, and then looked up at his father.

'Why did you want more money if you already had some?' the father grumbled.

'Because I didn't have enough, but now I do,' the little boy replied. 'Daddy, I have £20 now. Can I buy an hour of your time?'

'We think much more about the use of our money, which is renewable, than we do about the use of our time, which is irreplaceable.'
— *Jean-Louis Servan-Schreiber*

Every moment of your life, including this one, is a fresh start. – *B.J. Marshall*

A Creed To Live By

Don't undermine your worth by comparing yourself
with others.
It is because we are different that each of us is special.
Don't set your goals by what other people deem important.
Only you know what is best for you.

Don't take for granted the things closest to your heart.
Cling to them as you would your life, for without
them life is meaningless.
Don't let your life slip through your fingers by living
in the past or for the future.
By living your life one day at a time, you live all the
days of your life.

Don't give up when you still have something to give.
Nothing is really over until the moment you stop trying.
Don't be afraid to admit that you are less than perfect.
It is the fragile thread that binds us to each other.

Don't be afraid to encounter risks.
It is by taking chances that we learn how to be brave.

Don't shut love out of your life by saying it is
impossible to find.
The quickest way to receive love is to give love.
The fastest way to lose love is to hold it too tightly;
And the best way to keep love is to give it wings.

Don't dismiss your dreams.
To be without dreams is to be without hope;
To be without hope is to be without purpose.

Don't run through life so fast that you forget
Not only where you've been, but also where you're going.
Life is not a race, but a journey to be savoured each
step of the way.

— Nancye V. Sims

©1999 Nancye V. Sims. Reproduced with kind permission of Nancye V. Sims.

The hero is the one with ideas. – *Jack Welch*

Exercises

Wear an elastic band and ping it every time you use a negative word or phrase about yourself. That is, 'I can't', 'maybe', 'might', 'could have', etc.

Create your success journal and start using it today. Look at it every day and allow yourself to embrace your success. 'Coach' yourself to strive for success and stop when you hear your internal 'commentator' leading you towards failure.

CHAPTER TWO

The IMpact Code

M = Model from the best

Watch, learn, do, succeed

Model from the best – summary

Learn from your heroes.

Model your behaviour on your heroes.

What can you do today to be more like your heroes?

Focus on what you want, not what you don't want.

Plan for success.

You have to do it by yourself, but you can't do it alone.

Learn from the best

'Fake it till you make it!'

— Tony Robbins

Wise words indeed. But you don't believe it can work? Try
giving happiness a go and see what happens. If you are
feeling really low and can't be bothered to do anything,
force yourself to smile. Keep smiling, start humming and
think happy thoughts. Really, I'm not joking, give it a go.
You simply won't believe how powerful faking it can be.
Now, you know I am not talking about lying or cheating;
I'm talking about changing the way you act to emulate
either the feeling you want to create or the outcomes you
want to achieve (remember E+R=O). If you want to be
happy, make yourself happy. If you want to find love,
open you heart to love and start doing romantic things
for the one you love (without becoming a stalker!). If you
want more success in your job then start emulating the
behaviour of successful people. It isn't as difficult as it
sounds. After all, it didn't take much effort to smile, did
it?

We all need a hero. Who are your heroes? Why are they
your heroes? What is it that they do that inspires you so
much? Have you ever modelled your behaviour on theirs?

I always ask my audiences these questions and 90% of
them normally stare back blankly. We grown-ups don't
like to think about having 'heroes'. Isn't that another
activity for kids? Occasionally, someone will say Nelson
Mandela, Richard Branson and Bill Gates. When I ask
them why they said those names, they always say because
they are successful. You're right they are successful, but
not in the same ways. So, what is it about these people
that is so appealing?

Nelson Mandela has triumphed over incredible adversity
and through his fight for justice and equality has changed
the way the world understands racial dynamics; he is a
successful spiritual leader. Bill Gates and his organization
are undoubtedly responsible for changing the face of the
world. In terms of communication, no other organization has touched as many lives and businesses as Microsoft. Love it or hate it, Microsoft has changed the world
we live in and, for the most part, for the better. Richard
Branson is the kind of entrepreneur that everybody loves.

You can't get there from 'not here'. *Richard Moon*

His energy and business talent have created a global business that is known for its dedication to quality and customer service. He is also very likable and 'normal' and has a great sense of humour. We would all love to have his cash, but it is his personality that most people warm to.

But, think about these people in terms of their path to glory. Nelson Mandela ended up in jail, Richard Branson went bankrupt several times before he finally made it and Bill Gates struggled in the early years to make his ventures work. They have all had their fair share of disasters – success has not come easy for any of these people and I am sure they all would agree that along the way they have paid a high price for success. What separates them from the pack isn't their success, it's their ability to keep going. Dogged determination, a unique style and a clear philosophy that they 100% believed in, have enabled them to achieve such incredible success.

People latch on to these icons because they see their material wealth or global fame as noteworthy and, let's be honest, none of us is above feeling a little bit envious of incredible wealth. But what makes them special is

how they got there, not what they got in the end. Heroes
don't have to be famous or rich; if you admire a person
then that is enough to qualify them as your hero. You
might respect your local shopkeeper for the good work he
does in the community whilst still managing a 24-hour
business and a large family. How he lives his life is to be
admired and just because he isn't your typical candidate
for a bit of hero worship, doesn't mean you can't emulate
his behaviour to help improve your own life.

What makes your heroes special? Mandela is compassionate, Gates has conquered the universe with his incredible
capacity for innovation and Branson has turned risk-tak-
ing into a fine art. However, all of them share a few things
in common: determination, energy for their 'cause' and a
breathtaking capacity for hard work. But, above all else,
all three of these accomplished men are visionaries. They
saw their success, could imagine their world with success
and went for it.

In my opinion, if you want to be like your hero, you need
to start acting like them in your everyday life.

Nobody who ever gave his best regretted it. – *George Halas*

My hero is Stelios from easyJet. Not just because he took on the big names of the aerospace industry but because he starts every meeting in the same way. He asks everyone to stand in front of their chairs – he then asks them if the chair is empty or full. Perhaps an obvious response would be 'Duh, it's empty!' 'Well,' he says, 'your job is to fill it!'

What's the purpose of easyJet? Bums on seats.

So, when I talk about modelling I am not talking about making model airplanes, nor do I want you to lose half of your body weight and take up a new career on the cat-walk. No, what I want to talk about is learning to replicate the performance and behaviour of brilliant performers; be they in the workplace, sports, education or any other arena of life.

Inspiration to make courageous changes does not have to come from obvious sources; you can take your strength from anywhere and anyone you admire or respect. Life is rich with variety and we need to look to the entire universe of experience for our education – not just the people who work in our industry or live in the same social 'neighbourhood' as us. Modelling is key to understanding how to reshape the way we do things – there's no better way to feel comfortable about change than learning from someone else's experience.

So, ask yourself again, who are your role models and why? If you don't have any then it might explain why you are struggling to imagine what success might look and feel like. Our natural urge is to think about what we DON'T want. I don't want to get fat, I don't want to get hurt, and I don't want to be laughed at. Consequently, our focus is firmly directed on avoiding trouble. Fair enough, you might say, but where does that attitude lead us?

Let's take a quick look at how two different individuals consider the opportunity to speak in public. Public speaking is for many people a very scary prospect and one that often inspires genuine fear. But it isn't just a case of being afraid; the people who are afraid actually go through an entirely different thought process than those who aren't afraid. The differences are dramatic.

Inspiration and imagination go hand in hand.
– *Susan Fielder*

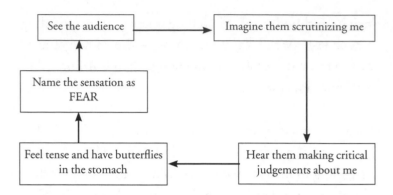

Model of a person who is afraid of public speaking.

Now let's look at what happens to the person who has a different model of thinking when it comes to speaking in public.

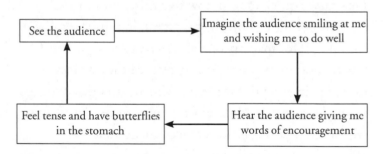

Model of person who has no fear of public speaking.

The difference is attitude and outlook, or in reality it is the extent to which we allow our own fear and negative self-image to dominate our behaviour. Remember, giving in to fear is natural; we're designed to live that way. Your job is to learn how to step outside that zone. Modelling your behaviour on someone who has achieved what you desire is a great way to help overcome your natural fear of change or risk.

If you compare the responses of the two public speakers, the one thing they share in common is fear (nerves). The difference is how they choose to respond to it – in most cases, people who have a deep-seated fear of public speaking avoid it at all costs. As we discussed earlier, visualizing success is a fast track to overcoming your initial fears (if you can imagine it, you can do it). But if you combine the power of your imagination to help create a positive emotional response to a scenario that would ordinarily frighten you, the results will be dramatic and quick. That is why modelling is so powerful.

Think again about the difference between how the two public speakers contemplated the same situation. One,

We can do more than belong, we can participate.
– *Maya Angelou*

the frightened speaker, is so worried about what might happen that he renders himself incapable of visualizing positive outcomes. Because we spend so long worrying about risk and dodging danger, we rarely take the time to focus on what we DO want. The outcome is simple. We get what we wish for. Avoiding trouble is not the same as getting a good result. Yes, the frightened speaker might opt out of the opportunity and as a result avoid the pain of rejection and failure. He did get what he wished for – no pain. However, what did he lose?

The reality of constantly focusing on the negative is that we usually end up with exactly what we were trying to avoid in the first place. I'm not saying that having a good attitude all of the time will guarantee your success, but it will change the way you deal with life's ups and downs. My life has been as crappy as it has been great, and I have a tremendous positive attitude. The difference is that I don't expect trouble, so when it comes (and it always will) I'm not totally defeated by it – I get over it and move on.

Modelling our behaviour on those who have achieved great success means that we have to acknowledge that the path to success is unlikely to run smoothly. However, maintaining a 'winning' attitude and behaviour patterns give us that all important 'bounce back' capability essential for long-term success.

Even though the concept of modelling has been around for centuries, it was in the 1970s that a young college student, Richard Bandler, discovered the work of Fritz Perls (The founder of Gestalt Therapy) and Virginia Satir (Family Therapy). So he decided to collaborate with a professor, John Grinder, from the University of California to find out why these two therapists got better results from their clients than many others of their peers.

They discovered that by finding out exactly how these two dynamic therapists did their work, they were able to copy their methods and get the same quality results. They went on to model Milton Erickson, a pioneering hypnotherapist, and published their first books, *The Structure of Magic* Volumes 1 and 2. These pioneering publications laid down the foundations of what was to become known today as Neuro Linguistic Programming, commonly referred to as NLP.

All the wonders you seek are within yourself.
– *Thomas Brown*

By exploring how leaders in their field go about their
work or play, they determined that it was possible for
almost anyone to get the same or similar results. In
the thirty years following their original work the word
modelling has become synonymous with the recognition
and transference of a skill set. This isn't just a theory, it's a
scientific fact: modelling works.

We begin modelling from a very early age. We've already
talked about when a child learns to walk. The baby sees
that the adults around him are able to move around much
quicker and more elegantly and so copies their behaviour;
he or she attempts the same actions. The main difference
between the child and adult is that the child does not give
up on his first attempt. He begins to realize what didn't
work the first few times and through a process of testing
eventually arrives at a solution for how to stand up on
two feet and walk. It reminds me of the Japanese proverb
'Failure is not falling down but refusing to get up'.

Modelling has been used to great success in many sales
organizations around the world. Sales people are natural modellers; they want to succeed and will adopt any

new behaviour that will enable them to win. Their fear is failure, so taking a chance on a new behaviour pattern is logical to them and they are by their very nature brave in the face of emotionally challenging situations. By researching what it is that their top performers do differently, sales organizations have been able to prepare a 'model' for success, which less successful individuals can then apply. You can apply the same approach to any aspect of your life. Find a person who has, in your opinion, succeeded in life and find out more about them and how they operate. In the case of the successful sales person, the questioning may have taken the following form.

1. What do you say to yourself before an important call or meeting?
2. What picture do you have in your mind?
3. What do you hear the customer saying?
4. What do you do if things go wrong?

Interestingly, the questions don't explore the 'how' of behaviour, but the 'what'. Most importantly, the emphasis is on attitude response rather than just a checklist of activity. That is why you can model your behaviour on people

Great things are done by a series of small things brought together. – Vincent Van Gogh

you admire from any area of life and business. It doesn't really matter what they achieve, but rather, it is what they do to help them achieve it that is important. We will look at what distinguishes a successful person from everyone else in the next chapter, but for now try to imagine how you would need to respond to help make your dreams reality. Ask yourself what makes up the core of your fear and what you need to do or think to overcome that fear and get back 'in the room'.

Search out people you admire and start listening. Find out how they describe situations or events and model their behaviour in the context of the success you want to create for yourself. Recognize what makes them different to you in terms of how they think and perform in difficult situations and learn from their experience. Use modelling as your emotional crutch as you learn to create IMPACT in your own life.

Remember: success leaves clues.

When I am running one of my Professional Speaker Boot Camps, the entire day is spent walking delegates through my own personal model of what I have had to do to build a successful speaking business – it is not about 'how' I did it, but what I had to do to enable my own success. Yes, you can apply some of the practical lessons from those people you chose to model from, but in essence you should be looking to model your thought processes on theirs, rather than simply trying to replicate the physical manifestations of their success. I know that the hopeful speakers who come along to my workshop can't possibly do everything that I have done, but they can learn how to be prepared, how to cope with rejection, how to believe in themselves and what works in terms of promoting themselves.

Every life is unique and there is no possible chance of replicating the success of, say, Richard Branson or Bill Gates. The world is a different place today than it was when they began to create their respective business empires, but we can learn a vast amount from them in terms of tenacity, commitment and positive attitude. Every successful person in the world has at some point been a failure. What separates individuals is not how many times they fall, but how fast they get back up and try again.

Change is not merely necessary to life, it is life. – Alvin Toffler

One of the biggest mistakes made in business today is the fact that many managers operate from a principle of 'do what I say' rather than 'do what I do', and this creates a culture of mistrust and apathy.

'Chris is such a loser, he says one thing and then goes right ahead and does another; if he can't be bothered to do it, why should we?'

Good point.

We are all guilty of this to a certain degree; it is so easy to see the logic of a situation and rationalize why we should do things differently, but overcoming our fear is quite a different prospect. To be successful – no matter what it is you want – demands that you learn to 'walk the talk'. When we say one thing and do another it is simply be-cause we are not passionate enough about the change to live up to the challenge of 'being the change'.

If you think you are passionate about something and you hear yourself saying 'I do love that, it's just that…' well, stop kidding yourself. Until you can say, 'I am going to try, I am going to succeed, I can do it,' don't bother trying to persuade anyone – especially yourself – that you want it. If you are genuinely passionate about something, there really isn't anything that can get in the way of success. Only you can make it, only you can break it.

Modelling is not only a great way to help build a structure around the behaviour you need to adopt to realize the change, it will inspire you to keep trying and teach you how to enlist the help of those around you.

Desire is possibility seeking expression.
– *Ralph Waldo Emerson*

Get the right kind of help

The General and the Boy

Once there was a general who wanted to cross a river. He was unsure of the depth of the river and whether his horse could make it across the river. He looked around for help and saw a little boy nearby. He asked the boy for advice. The boy looked at the size of the general's horse and paused for a moment. He then confidently told the general that it was safe for him and his horse to cross the river. The general proceeded to cross the river on his horse. As he approached the middle of the river, he suddenly realized that the river was, in fact, very deep, and he almost drowned. After he recovered from his shock he shouted at the boy and threatened to punish him. The boy was stunned and innocently replied, 'But General, I see my ducks crossing the river every day without any problem, and my ducks have shorter legs than your horse'.

The principles of successful modelling

If you need advice, get it from people who know what they are talking about. Napoleon Hill says that, 'opinion is the cheapest commodity on earth'. Make sure you review – for yourself – the opinions of others before you act on them. Consideration is the key. Remember to pause before you act. Not only will this help you resist the urge to run at the first sign of trouble, it will also give you time to make considered choices about the way you want to behave in order to make that change.

The story of Kriss Akabusi sums it up. When his 400m running career seemed to be over, but he was not ready to retire from athletics, he decided to try the 400m hurdles, which not only requires speed but grace and agility. He definitely had the speed to jump, but to jump gracefully was not natural for him; so he went to the USA to learn from the very best there was – the infamous Ed Moses.

The story's about you. – *Horace*

Ed Moses ran for ten years without losing a single race. He was the best there was, and probably still is, with an unblemished record. Kriss went to the USA at his own expense, spent many months and asked thousands of questions. The result of all his effort and determination was he that became one of the world's best, winning a bronze at the Olympics. He is still the British and European record holder.

What would you do if you thought your career was over? Would you ask more people for support or just accept that it was over?

My suggestion would be to do what Kriss did; find the best, allow yourself to be mentored, and run like hell!

> 'You have to do it by yourself, and you can't do it alone.'
>
> — *Martin Rutte*

Masterminding

It's a mistake to think that just because the 'more' we seek in life is a personal goal rather than a 'community' goal, we can't ask other people to help us. The truth is that we probably won't achieve even one per cent of what we want without other people. As we have already discussed, it is really important to model our behaviour on people we respect and trust. I am now working with my third Masterminding team and over the years I am certain that I would not have been able to develop my personal and business life without their help and support. My first team, which comprised Fran (my wife), Robin Siegar, Graham Davis and Roy Shepperd, supported me through the turbulent changes in my early career and helped me develop the concept of my speaking career.

With my second team, of which Fran was again a member, my focus was on developing an international business, so I worked with people who could support me in that. I worked with Betsy Haas, Debbie Wilny and Krista Buckner. This proved to be a winning combination for

That it will never come again is what makes life sweet.
– *Emily Dickinson*

me and helped me take my career to the next level in a remarkably short period of time.

Following on from this, I developed a new team in late 2004 with whom I still work: Shay McConnon, Steff Du Plessis and Steve Head. I have new goals and a clearer focus of what I want to achieve moving forward and I know that with the help of my team I can achieve my dreams. We all need heroes, but we also need a little help from our friends.

So, how do we recruit the important people we need to help us achieve our goals? Using the power of partnerships to manifest productivity and prosperity is nothing more than leveraging the combined energy of the people in your life to help you and, in turn, help them, along the way. We have already ascertained that you want to do better, so now it is time to start putting some meat on the bones of your grand plan for getting and giving more IMPACT.

It's time to make it happen.

Mastermind your success

Team play, team power, team everything! With the help of your friends and colleagues you can get everything you dreamed of. Maybe you just need regular emotional support, a critical review of your plan or practical 'hands-on' help to get the job done. As soon as you have sorted out your purpose guide (this is covered in detail in the next chapter) and broken down your life plan into bite-size chunks, you need to start getting to work on making it happen.

Not only can your personal Masterminding team help you achieve your new goals, they can also be there to help you retain your focus on other parts of your life that you don't want to affect or change. You have to make sure that chasing one dream doesn't leave another in ruins. How many successful people end up in divorce courts or devastated at the loss of their family? It always seems to happen

Who are 'they' that hold so much power over our lives?
– Orville Thompson

when they weren't looking…or were they just constantly absent from the room when they were with their family?

The team you select to help you with specific aspects of your plan should understand that a Masterminding team is not just about you and what you want; it is a mutual support team. You have already taken the most difficult step in acknowledging you need to change the way you live your life. So what now?

> 'The journey of a thousand miles begins with a single step.'
>
> *– Lao Tzu*

Setting your objectives

In the next chapter we will cover the need to sort out your purpose from your passion, and we have already discussed how to discern your Commentator from your Coach. But, to be the player we all want to be, we have to have a game plan in place to get us there. We all need goals (in every sense of the word) and the best way to achieve them is to write them down.

In order to get constructive help and support from other people it will help enormously if you can give them something to consider. The best thing to do is prepare your objectives and goals first and give them to each of the team members (we'll talk about how to recruit them later) as a guide. Each member of the team should share their personal goals with the rest of the team. No good keeping it all a secret! How the devil do you expect anyone to help you if they don't know what it is you are after?

Change takes guts. It takes imagination.
It takes commitment. – *John Taylor*

Why should I set goals?

What makes people do what they do? What fears do they have? What is it that makes some people live an incredible life while others with the same opportunities seem to squander their lives away? How can we help people move from grovelling to greatness?

Have you ever noticed someone who has no goals? They typically are not DOING anything! When they are at home they probably lie around and watch television all the time. When they are at work they hardly ever contribute any new, positive ideas – yet they are probably the first ones to criticize anyone else's suggestions. They tend to resist change, and it shows! These are the people who are detrimental to the company because of the way they treat customers and other staff members.

In a social environment, people with no goals are usually the ones who complain about everything and tell you about all their aches and pains. They are always whining about how badly life has treated them. The rally cry of a person who has no goals is, 'I'm bored!'

- If you're casual about your goals, you'll end up a casualty.
- Creating IMPACT is a constant, never-ending process.
- Working on your life is a constant, never-ending process.
- The quality of your life will largely depend on the quality of your goals.
- Whether your goals are reached or not will largely depend on your actions.
- Whether you take action or not will largely depend on your desire and commitments.
- Whether you keep your commitments or not will largely depend on who you commit to.
- Who you commit to will largely depend on faith, trust and love.
- When faith, trust and love exist, your life becomes a masterpiece!
- Start developing your masterpiece by combining your goals, your actions and your commitments with faith, trust and love!

Make it happen!

What you can't out of, get into wholeheartedly.
– *Mignon McLaughlin*

Picking your team

If you follow any type of sports, you may have heard
successful teams talking about their team's 'chemistry'.
Anyone who has had the opportunity to play any team
sport will know exactly what I'm talking about when I
say that having the right chemistry on your team can
make you into winners. I don't necessarily mean winning
the game itself, although this kind of win does produce
a great feeling of triumph. I mean winning on a much
broader framework.

In order to fulfill its potential, a team needs a cross-sec-
tion of skills and personalities. Not everyone can be the
centre forward for their team. If everyone were the centre
forward, who would look after defence, or support on the
wings? Likewise, not everyone can be pitchers on baseball
teams, goalies on hockey teams, etc., etc.

A range of personal qualities is essential, too. Some team
members are great leaders who inspire others around
them and raise them to higher levels than they could nor-

mally reach. Other members of the team are quieter but still contribute in important ways. Each member of a successful team will bring unique qualities to the table. With the right blend of leadership, motivation and – above all else – action, the team will have many successes.

Effective coaches understand that it takes a good blend of people to work together, and will select team members with diverse backgrounds and experiences. The coach's job is to channel each team member's skills and energy towards common goals. A solid blend of different personalities is what makes any kind of team enterprise exciting, challenging and fun – whether in sports, work, partnerships or marriage. I guess this is why we hear the phrase 'opposites attract' so often.

My personal assistant and I work well together because she tends to be more process-oriented and enjoys taking projects through to fruition, whilst I possess tremendous creativity, have non-stop ideas and energy, and know how to have fun. While we each have all of the personality types within us, usually one or two personality traits tend to dominate our actions.

To find an open road, have an open mind. – *John Towne*

For this reason, when you seek out prospective members to become part of your Mastermind group, it's wise to look for a variety of people, not just people who are like you. This is not to say that a group of people with similar personalities working together will not achieve results, but they may not consider a whole range of useful options that someone with a different personality might suggest. The main reason to seek out various personalities for your group is so that you will have different perspectives brought forward and therefore will be able to see things from all angles. For example, perhaps at one of your meetings you express some difficulty in achieving a particular goal. Another member in your group might say, 'Have you tried this or have you tried that?' and you may hear some great ideas that you had not considered at all before then.

Quantum-leap your results

Let me share a personal example. It's a familiar story; you may have heard it before and it starts like this: I'm writing a book…

We all have a 'project'; something that nags away at us and yet we never seem to get around to realizing our dreams. For me, it was writing a book; it took me a very long time to get my act together but when I did the results were amazing. In the end it wasn't as difficult as I had feared and I was amazed how easily it all came together. Here is the simple formula I used to Quantum-leap the results in every area of my life. With a little practice you could achieve the same kind of success and get that book written or climb that mountain. Quantum-leaping your life works!

DESIRE + DEADLINE + FOCUS + MASSIVE ACTION + MASTERMIND COMMITMENT = SUCCESS

You can do anything – but you can't do everything.
– *David Allen*

That is the formula for Quantum-leaping your results.

In order to give you a full appreciation of the way the equation works, let's examine each component of the formula as it relates to this particular story.

Desire

Make a good solid list of reasons why you want what you say you want. The more reasons you have to accomplish the goal, the more likely you are to achieve the results you want. When your 'whys' are strong enough, your 'whats' begin to happen!

Deadline

Make sure that you pick a deadline that will make you stretch yourself so that you can truly enjoy and benefit from the process of Quantum-leaping. Be sure not to overdo it; don't set a time limit that is so close it will frustrate you and discourage you. Just as importantly, don't set a time that is so far away that there is no challenge and you will lose interest.

Focus

When you are in the room, be in the room! I realize that you will have many other things going on in the world when you begin your process. Handle what needs to be handled and complete any obligations or commitments that you have made. FOCUS on the task at hand – and GET BUSY!

Massive Action + Mastermind Commitment

There is no holding back now! Make your commitments to your Mastermind partners. Ask for commitments in return if you need them. Remember, you are in a Quantum-leap process and you need every bit of assistance that you can get. There are two main questions that you should keep asking yourself throughout the Quantum-leap process.

1. What end result am I looking for?
2. What is my next step?

So, what's the next step in your Quantum leap?

People can't answer a call that isn't made. – *Robert Morgan*

In Napoleon Hill's classic book, *Think and Grow Rich*, he
talks about a union of individuals who want to help each
other achieve whatever they want by focusing their skills
through a Mastermind alliance. The process of combining and focusing enables them to meet their dreams. A
new, more powerful mind is created when two or more
individuals work together in harmony and focus.

The world is shrinking. Not physically, but because
of our ability to travel to any place around the globe,
literally in hours. We can travel across countries, conti-
nents and great oceans in aeroplanes at speeds that were
thought impossible 100 years ago. Cargo and food sup-
plies can be air-lifted to countries in need. Peace-keeping
troops can quickly move anywhere in the world to help
restore peace and harmony in troubled countries.

All of this is possible because of the Mastermind partner-
ship of Orville and Wilbur Wright. The Wright brothers
are famous for their belief that man could fly. Where

would we be without their Mastermind alliance? You never know where or how your Mastermind partner(s) will come into your life. Like anything else, when you plant the seed of a goal in your mind, events and circumstances magically unfold to help you achieve what you want.

Mastermind partners are awesome! Combined, they can make a tangible difference in your world and the world at large.

Where the attention goes, energy flows, and results show.

Everyone thinks of changing the world, but no one thinks of changing himself. – *Leo Tolstoy*

Exercises

Write an article about your hero and consider how you can apply lessons you have learned from them to your own life. Write the article from the point of view of sharing your ideas with people in your team so that they can understand what you admire and how your hero could help them too.

Read the autobiography of your main hero. Ask yourself what that person did well and what you would have done differently. You never know, you might know more than your hero!

Spend an entire day acting as if you were your hero and notice how much more confidence it gives you.

CHAPTER THREE

The ImPact Code

P = Passion & purpose

Chase your passion, not
your pension

Passion – summary

If you aren't going to be passionate about it, don't do it.

Don't deny your dreams.

Chase your passion, not your pension.

Find purpose in your passion; let your purpose be your passion.

If what you are doing right now is not in alignment with the bigger picture then stop doing it.

Surround yourself with passionate people.

Eradicate negative people and influences from your life.

The man in the mirror

When you get what you want
In your struggle for self
And the world makes you
King for the day.

Just go to a mirror and look at yourself
And see what
THAT man has to say.

For it isn't your mother or father or wife
Whose judgement you must pass,
The fellow whose verdict counts most in your life,
Is the one staring back from the glass.

Some people may think you're a straight-shooting chum
And call you a wonderful friend,
But the man in the glass says you're only a bum,
If you can't look him straight in the eye.

He's the fellow to please, never mind all the rest
For he is with you clear up to the end,
And you've passed your most dangerous difficult test,
If the man in your glass is your friend.

You may fool the whole world down the pathway of life,
And get pats on your back as you pass,
But your final reward will be heartache and tears,
If you're cheating the man in the glass.

— Dale Wimbrow

Use your imagination not to scare yourself to death but to
inspire yourself to life – *Adele Brookman*

Passion and purpose

I love playing tennis. In fact, my first 'real' job was as a
tennis pro, coaching kids. So, tennis has always been very
important to me. Not just because I love the game, but
also because it has taught me so much about dedication
and what winning is really all about. One of my favourite
tennis players – Andre Agassi – is my hero for reasons
other than his prowess on a tennis court. Agassi picked
up a tennis racquet at the age of two and his dream was to
be the number one player in the world. Despite on-court
tantrums and well documented off-court antics he finally
made it.

Like so many before him, after struggling a lifetime
to achieve his goal, when he made it he lost focus and
started to drift. In a surprisingly short period of time, his
ranking started to slip and eventually took him all the
way down to number 141. He could have given up, but
instead he chose to win again. Achieving what you have
always dreamed of is often not quite what you expect and

unless you visualize and plan for success it can easily slip through your fingers. Agassi lost grip of his dream and lost it all.

More than anything else, it was the loss of his drive to win that ultimately cost him his dream; he didn't know where to go next and so he started to fall back. He was lost inside the reality of his own 'dream come true'. To be more exact he had allowed himself to lose sight of why he used to win. He came to his senses and realized that he wanted success again, but he knew that it was going to be a long, painful road back to the top. He had to fight to get back into the habit of winning, of wanting to win. Given how far he had fallen, it was something that very few people would have the courage to do. He was determined. Dropping down a league, to the Challenger Series, and playing in front of crowds of between 1 and 20 against opponents ranked 120–1000, he clawed his way back into the game; this time with renewed purpose and newly ignited passion.

He did not go back to basics, he went forward to basics (Peter Thompson, a good friend, taught me that). Within 18 months he was back at number one, married to Steffi

If you want to do something, you find a way. If you don't want to do something, you find an excuse. – *Dawn Bauer*

Graff and had enough sponsorship to guarantee his future. He remains a top-ten player today, long after most of his contemporaries have retired and are playing in the Seniors' League. He is everything a winner should be: passionate, determined and humble.

What do you do when your sales are slipping, or your kid is constantly misbehaving and getting into trouble at school? Do you start doubting your abilities and avoid the issue (most of us are expert at distracting ourselves from the task in hand) or do you give up? It's not always easy to give up – especially if the problem is your child, but you can give in to doubt and give up in your heart long before you give up the physical effort. The effects can be devastating on you and everyone around you.

If what you are doing is truly your passion, could anything stop you from doing it? Just one thing: you. Without passion, purpose means nothing. Without purpose, passion is utterly wasted.

Chase your passion, not your pension

We all know that if we follow our hearts we won't regret what we do, but how many of us actually do anything about it? Is how you spend your days the way you would like to spend them, or is it how you feel you 'have' to live your life? Are you in a self-imposed life sentence of making ends meet? If you are living a life without real passion then you have given in to laziness. You're done.

Responsibility is not an excuse for giving up on our dreams, but it is the one we all tout as the root cause of malaise. 'I'd love to do that, but how can I when I have got the kids, the mortgage and then there's retirement to take care of?' Living today is a very tiring business and the energy it takes – or so it would seem – to make changes is often overwhelming. My God, how would you go about changing your career without jeopardizing your family's security?

> What you will do matters. All you need is to do it.
> – *Judy Grahn*

If your dream is to be a potter and you are the CEO of a large corporation, the shift in income would be unbearable. I'm a realist; I know what giving up financial security is all about – I lost it all once and I know what it feels like to worry about where your next meal is coming from.

Even when my life was turned upside down I still had something to shoot for. I didn't care that I was driving my Bentley around (yes, I was the original 1980s yuppie) as a taxi cab. I would have cleaned the streets and flipped burgers if that is what it would have taken me to get back on track. I had a plan, I had a purpose, and I was and am completely passionate about what I want from life. Step by step, I changed the way I lived. I managed to keep my house, I put my kids through school and together, as a family, we are all living the lives we want. We did it together. It took compromise and patience, but in the end I have got where I wanted to be at this point in my life.

If throwing pots is what you want to do, get organized. Get some purpose in your life and start following your passion. You may well be financially secure, you might not: it doesn't matter. You can be just as trapped in your life when you have all the money you need, as you are when you have nothing. The point is, if you are that CEO who longs to toil over a potter's wheel, the pain of not having that in your life is probably crippling you emotionally. The same would be true if you were an at-home mum or dad and you dreamed of being a lawyer. The change may seem too big to achieve, but your dream really is worth chasing, because you are truly worthy of your dreams.

For many, sacrificing a dream is a very private misery, as most people are frightened to share their dreams with their family for fear of unbalancing them. Imagine how much better you would feel going to work each day if you knew that working in that job was just one part of your life plan to get you in front of that wheel? Your family will more than likely embrace the fact that you want to do that (if they don't, then you need to ask why not), they can help you get there, one step at a time. Earn enough to build your own studio – even if it takes ten years – and maybe while you are doing it go and lease time in an

All we can ask in our lives is that perhaps we can make a little
difference in someone else's. – *Lillian Davis*

established studio so that you can throw pots while you wait. Spend your time wisely, study from masters, learn your craft, build up a portfolio, and exhibit your works. Gradually, over time you will realize your dream. You will not have compromised the security of your family, but you will have lived your life for you as well as them. When you are old they won't thank you if you tell them you gave up on yourself for them. Nobody would want that on their conscience.

One of my dear friends is tormented by the fact that her mother loves to paint, has always wanted to paint, but just wouldn't do it. Even now, retired and financially secure she won't spend the money she worked so hard to acquire on her dream of painting. She insists that she is saving it for the inheritance she thinks she needs to leave to her family. I can understand that kind of commitment – anyone with kids can – but when your kids are pleading with you to 'spend it, live your life, leave nothing but good memories behind,' what could she be waiting for?

After many long months of persuading she has finally started to take art classes and her success is beginning to drive her on. In the end, maybe it wasn't the fear of her children's security that kept her back. Maybe it was the fear that she couldn't do the very thing she loved and that would be too much to bear after all this time of dreaming about it.

Chasing your dreams, no matter how small the daily steps you may take to get there, is a scary, emotionally risky business. Remember why we don't want to step outside our comfort zone. Is what you are currently working on worth giving up on yourself for? Even your kids aren't worth that. Blaming everyone else for your sacrifice is a nonsense that has to stop right now.

Think back through the years and ask yourself who you remember and why? Apart from your family and friends, the people we tend to remember are normally those individuals who are filled with energy and enthusiasm for life. People who live for themselves make incredible life partners.

If it hurts when you think about the fact that you aren't doing the thing you love or living the life you have always

When heart and skill work together expect a masterpiece.
– C. Reade

dreamed about, then you owe it yourself and everyone else in your life to change. Do you think you would be a happier person if you were living for your dreams? I would bet my house on the fact that you would be a better person to live with. You may never reach your goal, but the value of your life will increase exponentially when you start living for your dreams.

When people free themselves creatively, everything else miraculously starts to improve. Happiness breeds success. When you chase your passion, your pension will very likely take care of itself. At work, people might come to know you as the 'mad potter', but they will respect you for having a go and for doing things differently. You never know, you might inspire them to try something for themselves. Creating IMPACT in your life means teaching people how to treat you, which in turn means showing them all the good things about living the way you live.

If you can demonstrate as a CEO that it is OK to have a passion other than your work and that it is possible to manage both successfully, imagine what that would do for the people who work in your company? Just think how much productivity would increase if only an extra 25% of your staff came to work happier because in the evening they lived for themselves and when they came to work, they were 'in the room' and working through that part of their life plan.

We can all share in the positive energy of following our passion. Dreams should not be confined to the privacy of your own heart. Like a lost love or a missed opportunity, living without passion can haunt you forever. Don't do that to yourself. Acknowledge your past, park it, then embrace your dreams and let passion flow through your veins. Tomorrow does not have to feel like today. Start living right now. Just say to yourself, 'my name is John, I am a CEO, I am a dad, but really I am a potter.'

Finding purpose in all that passion

Dreaming alone won't get you where you want to be. It takes work; hard work and determination to make your dreams come true – no matter how grand or modest they are. It takes guts to step up and be counted for what you really want in life. Even if your passion in life is your kids and all you want is more respect from them – you have the power to get that. Respect is earned; maybe you haven't been making the right kind of 'deposits' in their emotional piggy banks lately. Would they love you any less if you shared your dreams with them, even asked them to help you? There is nothing wrong in asking for help – even from our kids. They will love you for it. That doesn't mean you can lean on your kids, but asking a person to give your their love and support is empowering for everyone concerned.

If you need to make time for your family, then you have to discover how to do it without compromising the other things you like about your life. Life is about compromise, but that should never be at the expense of the quality of your own life.

'That's easy for you to say!'

Not really. I still wrestle with the balance between what I want and what I have to do to keep my family alive and well, but I have found my passion and purpose. My family is part of that and I know that getting what I want means giving them what they want – my purpose is my passion and vice versa. I don't begrudge the time I have to spend doing things I don't really enjoy, because I get to do so many of the things I really want and often it is my family who benefit from the things I would rather not do. I feel content, even in the face of disaster, because I make sure I learn how to move on. The only successful way to embrace your passion is to get a basic 'plan' – have a purpose.

Like all the books on time management tell us, break your task down into bite-size pieces and you will get it done. Spend too long thinking about the enormity of the whole task and you won't get anything done. The same is

It is not who is right, but what is right, that is of importance.
– *Thomas Huxley*

true of making changes. You can't do it all in one night; anything worth doing is worth toiling for. Yes, we need to visualize success, but we also need to imagine completing the small steps that will get us where wc long to be.

Finding your purpose doesn't necessarily mean creating a detailed project plan that has to be worked out each week in detail (but it would be another great way to put off change … imagine the hours you could spend working out your life plan!). Finding your purpose is much easier than that.

Here is a quick exercise which might help you get there. Write down the answers to the following in the front of your new success journal.

- What is my passion?
- What are my bite-size goals?
- What mechanism will help me get there?
- What Action do I need to take?
- What will the result look like?
- Is this my truth?

When you have the answers to these, you will have your purpose guide. Don't burden yourself with unrealistic time lines. Just know roughly where you need to be and start working towards it. Successful people have many things in common and we can learn a thing or two from looking at what makes them tick.

These are the five things you'll find every successful and passionate person has in common:

1. They have a dream
2. They have a plan
3. They have specific knowledge or training
4. They're willing to work hard
5. They don't take 'no' for an answer.

Remember: success begins with a state of mind. You must believe you will be successful in order to become a success. Visualize it.

The following is a list of the skills, talents and characteristics you'll find in people who make an IMPACT.

I think the one lesson that I have learned is that there is no substitute for paying attention. *Diane Sawyer*

- Passionate people have a dream and a very well-defined purpose.
- They have a definite goal.
- They know what they want.
- They are not easily influenced by the thoughts and opinions of others.
- They have willpower.
- They have ideas.
- Their strong desire produces powerful results.
- They go out and do things that others say can't be done.

Remember: it only takes one sound idea to achieve success.

Remember: people who excel in life are those who produce RESULTS not REASONS.

Anybody can come up with excuses and explanations for why they haven't made it; those who want to succeed badly enough don't make excuses.

Passionate people have genuine enthusiasm. They want to accomplish something. They have energy, commitment and pride. They have self-discipline. They are willing to work hard and to go the 'extra mile'. They have a burning desire to succeed. They are willing to do whatever it takes.

Remember: with hard work come results. The joy in life comes from working towards a goal and achieving something as a result.

Remember: some people are so poor they can't pay attention.

Passionate people are highly motivated towards achievement. They take great satisfaction in accomplishing a task.

Passionate people are focused. They concentrate on their main goals and objectives. They don't get side-tracked. They don't procrastinate. They work on the projects that are important, and don't allow those projects to sit until the last minute. They're productive, not just busy.

They work on Number 1.

If you can't do it with feeling, don't. – *Patsy Cline*

Passionate people learn how to get things done. They use their skills, talents, energy and knowledge to the fullest extent. They do the things that need to be done, not just the things they like to do. They are willing to work hard and to commit themselves to getting the job done.

Remember: happiness is found in doing and accomplishing, not in owning and possessing.

Passionate people take responsibility for their actions. They don't make excuses. They don't blame others and they don't whine and complain.

Passionate people look for solutions to problems. They're opportunity-minded; when they see opportunities they take advantage of them.

Passionate people make decisions. They think about the issues and relevant facts, give them adequate deliberation and consideration, and make a decision. Decisions aren't put off or delayed, they're made now!

Success tip: spend a little more time thinking and planning before you make your decision, and you'll make better decisions. But make sure you make the decision.

Success tip: when you don't get the expected results from the decision you've made, change your course of action. Decisions should never be carved in stone.

Passionate people have the courage to admit they've made a mistake. When you make a mistake, admit it, fix it, and move on. Don't waste a lot of time, energy, money, and/or other resources trying to defend a bad decision.

Remember: when people are wrong, they may admit it to themselves. If they are handled gently and tactfully, they may admit it to others and even take pride in their frankness and broad-mindedness. But people become very defensive and angry when others try to cram their mistakes down their throats.

Passionate people are self-reliant. They have the skills, talent and training that is needed in order to be successful.

A single idea can transform a life, a business,
a nation, a world. – *Dan Zadra*

Passionate people have specific knowledge, training and/ or skills and talents. They know the things they need to know to be successful. And when they need information, knowledge or skills and talents that they don't possess, they find someone who possesses them.

Passionate people work with and co-operate with other people. They have positive, outgoing personalities. They surround themselves with people who offer them help, support and encouragement. They are leaders.

Passionate people are enthusiastic. They're excited by what they're doing and that excitement is contagious. They draw people to them because these people want to work with them, do business with them and be with them.

Many years ago I was asked, 'Nigel, do you like pleasing habits or pleasing results?' As I pondered that probing question and squirmed in my chair like a worm at the end

of a hook, I felt as if I had painted myself into a corner.
A few moments later I answered, 'I like pleasing results.'
From that moment on my life changed. I began to do
the things that were difficult, because they enabled me to
achieve my goals.

It's one thing to unearth your dreams and put them on
paper, it's quite another to put them into action. Keep
your dream in your waking consciousness; learn to enjoy
imagining your success and how you will achieve it.
Constantly ask yourself, 'is what I am doing right now
going to get me where I need to be?' If it isn't then you
have to ask yourself why you are doing it. That is not the
same thing as doing things that might not 'light your
fire' if they need to be done to make your dream a reality.
If the only means you have to make money to feed your
kids and pay the bills is a drag, then the only way to bear
the wait until you reach your goal is to keep that goal in
mind.

Goodness is easier to recognize than to define. – *W H Auden*

You might say to yourself, 'Yes this sucks, I hate being a CEO, but tonight I have got a pot to throw in preparation for my first amateur exhibition, and it keeps my family safe and warm.' When the more tedious things in life are positioned correctly it is amazing how much extra energy you can find for them. Most of the time the only reason we really hate doing something is because there is nothing else going on in our lives worth 'living for'.

Make a promise to yourself that you will create a life you think is worth really 'living' in.

Surround yourself with passionate people

In the previous chapter we talked about getting help, setting goals and looking to others for inspiration. But there are a few words of caution. Even though most people are good, not everyone is good for *you*. I'm talking about the people who literally suck the life out of you. I'm talking about psychic vampires.

I say it all the time and I mean it: most people want you to succeed. I have a phenomenal team that supports me – they are all great. But I also know that if one of the team is having a crappy time, it could easily bring the rest of us down even though they want me and everyone else in the team to succeed. Why?

When faced with difficult situations, most people find it very hard to maintain their 'pep'. The problem isn't that they want to sabotage our effort; it's that they are bummed out and we can empathize with their plight.

Don't wait to be discovered. – *Gil Atkinson*

With retreating 'pep' levels they descend into gloom
and everyone quickly follows unless you do something
to interrupt the flow. My team copes because we have
recognized this as a potential team killer and take action
to prevent the rot from spreading when one of us is struggling.

People who want the best for you but are in a bad place
can be helped without destroying your own energy levels.
When one of our number is down we pull together and
use our combined energy to help pull them out of their
gloom and come up with practical solutions to their
problem. It makes us all feel better and gets the stricken
teammate back on track (that is the real wonder of masterminding!).

But imagine if one of your team does not want you to
succeed – what would happen to your energy levels then?

There are two groups of people in our lives; those who
support you to greatness or those who want to rain on
your parade (remember the quote – 'if you want the rain-
bow, you gotta put up with the rain.' – Dolly Parton).

One set of your friends or work colleagues are loving, nurturing, caring, supporting and the type of people who you could call at 3 a.m. in a real emergency and who would drop everything to support you. How many people have you got on your 'team' like that?

Then there is the other set of 'friends', the people who, when you see their number come up on caller display, your heart sinks because you know they are going to drain your energy and dump on you. Psychic vampires: just as deadly as the blood-sucking variety but not so easy to defend yourself against. Or so you might think.

These people literally suck the energy out of your body and for half an hour after the telephone call you still feel lethargic and it's as if all of your passion for life has been drained away. They, on the other hand, are fine. Having dumped and cleansed they move on to their next victim.

They really are your biggest competitors in business and in life come to think of it. At work these are the people who at 5.29 p.m. don't answer the telephone because it is not their client or who accidentally-on-purpose do not forward an important email to you. I liken them to weeds

Learning is not compulsory, but neither is survival.
– W. Edwards Deming

in your garden: they suck the oxygen out of the plant and very soon, without you even realizing it, they have taken over.

Here's the thing they all share in common. Most psychic vampires would rather be right than be happy. The fact is that unless you learn to deal with these 'terrorists' they will continue, in a very subtle way, to bring you or your 'team' down.

As I tell my audiences, if you are the manager or leader you have to learn to recognize them and then you have a choice: either inspire them or fire them. You cannot allow internal terrorists to carry on without consequence. If you do you are sending a very dangerous and clear message that their behaviour is acceptable.

Not only is that bad for them (in the long term), it is a disaster for you and every other member of your team. No point planning to take action and make an IMPACT in the world if you can't deal with energy-sucking, life-crushing, internal terrorists. Phil McGraw put it very eloquently when he said, 'we teach people how to treat us'.

So, if you are struggling to decide which step to take first, now you have it on a plate. Make your first action point to deal with the psychic vampires who live in your 'space'. With these people either eradicated from your life or contained, taking the second step on your path to success will be a lot easier. Try to remember that they are just as messed up as you are – they are just dealing with it differently. So, in fact, putting them straight about their behaviour is probably the kindest thing you could do for them and for yourself. Teaching them how to treat you is taking positive action and preventing them from sabotaging your plans or your health.

If you worry at the thought of a confrontation you should think of it this way. Maybe their behaviour is a result of some bad habits they have acquired in order to compensate for some scary stuff in their own world. Your first step could also be their first step towards making better choices about life as well. The most important consideration for you is that you have decided that their behaviour is unacceptable and you have to do something to change the influence they have on your life. If the relationship you have with the vampire isn't working for you, take steps to change it.

'We cannot become what we want to be
by remaining what we are.' – *Max Dupree*

So, next time your heart sinks when you hear that a vampire is waiting to talk to you on line one, or when yet another co-worker has been upset by your resident 'internal terrorist' – you have a choice. Take affirmative action.

Dealing with vampires is difficult, but not impossible. None of us wants to hurt another person, but more often than not the person causing you problems is unlikely to have considered your feelings. So, take the call, but tell them what is OK and what isn't. When they start to talk you into a slump, stop them and say, 'Look, I empathize with your situation but I find these conversations very difficult and I would prefer not to talk about these things any more. I am not saying I don't want to help you, but your situation is having a bad effect on me.' If they persist or get angry then you have to swallow hard and tell them straight. 'I value our past relationship, but this just isn't working for me and I think it is better that for both of us that I bow out and say goodbye.' Then hang up. You won't believe how empowering it is to take care of yourself.

If your problem person isn't a friend but a colleague then you have to take proper steps to advise them that their behaviour is unacceptable (no matter how uncomfortable it might seem at first) and if things don't improve – leave or make them leave. Whichever is best for the business or your life.

Don't hang around hoping they will change – they won't unless something changes for them. Whether your problem at work is your boss, his boss or the bitter receptionist who terrorizes you every time you walk through the door, take affirmative action. Speak to their boss is you have to, but take action to improve the situation. Don't let another day go by without eradicating the vampires from your life.

One day, with life and heart, is more than enough to find a world. – *James Russell Lowell*

Tell the total truth faster

The greatest legacy we can leave our children or the world we live in is the lesson that living a passionate life is worth more than any material gain we could ever hope to achieve. Being selfish and following your dreams will open up your life to incredible highs but it will teach everyone around you to do the same. Life's balance and ultimately our happiness, depends on our ability to follow our hearts; to be true to ourselves. Being honest is the key to living with passion. As I have already said, not everything we have to do is enjoyable, but becomes bearable when we live 'out in the open'. If it hurts, say it, explain why, and find a way with your friends and family to put it right. But, chase your dreams and never lose sight of what you want. No matter how crazy people may think you are, it's your dream not theirs, so it's up to you to live up to it.

In every situation you must tell the truth – even if it hurts the other person. Learn tact rather than the art of deception. Learn to love yourself enough to forgive yourself for wanting something different to the things you have got (it doesn't necessarily mean you don't value what you have; it might just mean that you want MORE).

Creating IMPACT demands integrity. The only way to realize your dreams and enjoy both the journey and the result is to live your life with passion, purpose and, above all else, integrity.

TELL THE TOTAL TRUTH FASTER.

Can anything be sadder than work unfinished? Yes, work never begun. – *Christina Georgina Rossetti*

Who says you can't?

Evelyn Glennie is renowned as the first lady of solo percussion. She performs 120 concerts each year and has recorded nine albums. Evelyn is profoundly deaf.

She started to lose her hearing at the age of 10 and due to severe nerve damage was profoundly deaf by the time she was 12. Her goal was to become a percussion soloist and in order to perform she learned to 'hear' music differently from others. She played in stockinged feet and could tell the pitch of a note by the vibrations she felt through her body and her imagination.

She applied to the prestigious Royal Academy of Music in London and despite opposition to her admission by some teachers was finally admitted and went on to graduate with the academy's highest honours.

Just because her doctor had made a diagnosis that she was profoundly deaf, it did not mean that her passion could not be realized.

'Follow your passion, follow your heart. They will lead you to the place you want to go.'

— *Evelyn Glennie*

Person to person, moment to moment, as we love, we change the world. – *Samahria Lyte Kaufman*

Exercise

Ask yourself the following questions and write down your instinctive answers – don't stop until you have finished all of the answers.

- Am I living my passion?
- What excites me?
- This is not a dress rehearsal; am I living the life I deserve?
- What do I believe in?
- In what guiding principles can I become constructively obsessed?
- What governs my life?
- What do I stand for?
- What puts meaning in my life?
- What qualities are important for my life to be complete?

When you have finished brainstorming your answers, go back and take a long time to consider each point. Explore why you wrote your answers and think about what you need to do to make them different or better? When you are done, write them up in a formal document and make that the beginning of your 'life plan'.

Determine that the thing shall be done, and then we shall
find the way. – *Abraham Lincoln*

CHAPTER FOUR

The ImpAct Code

A = Action

When all is said and done, much more is said than done

Action – summary

Get off your ass.

Do something now, what are you waiting for?

Share your dreams, live your dreams.

Break your goals down into bite-size chunks and start working on them immediately.

Seize every opportunity.

Learn from every mistake and every success.

Action

'When all is said and done, much more is said than done.'
How true is that? We're all big talkers, big dreamers, but
so often when it comes down to making things different
we find a million different reasons why we shouldn't do
the very thing we know will make us happy. Why? What
is it that keeps our dreams at arm's length? Well, we have
already talked about the past and how that can affect our
ability to be in the room. We know that our brain will
try to keep us out of harm's way, but that isn't the whole
answer.

Chasing our dreams is scary – I think I've made that
point pretty clear. The trouble is, making your dreams
a reality takes effort and most of the time, people just
can't be bothered. The bottom line is that even though
we say we want things to be different, we don't want it
bad enough to do anything about it. You will probably
say that it isn't that simple. Sure, life is difficult; there's
the kids, the job, the house, the family, the lawn to mow,
the shopping to get, the bills to sort out. When are you

supposed to find time to live differently in the middle
of all that? Well, if you can't find time to make your life
more valuable and enjoyable for yourself then stop whining about it. Shut up. Get on with the drudgery of your
life and rejoice in it. If you don't have the energy to take
action to make your life different then it must be pretty
good as it is. So, what's the problem?

The problem is that you don't want your life to keep
going the same way. You're reading this book, aren't you?
You're trying to find a way to make a difference, but what
you really want is for someone to tell you how to make
your life perfect without ever having to lift a finger. Well,
today is your lucky day; here's the piece of advice you
have been waiting for. The very thing you need to know
to make your life work in an instant.

You've gotta G.O.Y.A.

Still haven't got it? OK, here it is in plain English. GET
OFF YOUR ASS.

Life is work. Get over it.

> We think caged birds sing, when indeed they cry.
> – *John Webster*

Everybody worries about getting started. They put the blame on not enough time, too many responsibilities, but in truth most of the time we are all just frightened of failure. What if we work really hard, make the changes and our life isn't what we hoped it would be? That's a tough one, no doubt about it. Let me state the absolute obvious truth for you. So what? If you gave it your best shot and it didn't work out, then you will never regret it. No-regrets living means following your heart (even when it takes you down a different path to the one you set out to follow).

We've already talked about the fact that winning isn't usually what people expect it to be. Being successful is more often about how you fight for your cause, rather than the cause itself. It's the journey, not the destination that really makes the IMPACT in your life. A great life is worth working for.

Your dream might be to make contact with the family you were separated from many years ago. So, you get started and eventually you track them all down only to discover that you can't stand them once you got to know them. Would that be a failure? Of course not; at least you would know the answers to your questions. How much

would you have learned along the way? Yeah, sure you
might be disappointed that the family life you dreamed
of just isn't possible because your real family are a bunch
of maniacs, but maybe you might take a different view
on what makes a good family having made that journey?
You'll never know unless you try.

The law of universe is simple. Every action is rewarded
with an outcome. Positive thinking can only help you
deal with life; it can never make your life happen. Only
action will get you what you want. I promise you that
making even the smallest steps will have an incredibly
positive IMPACT on your life. So what are you waiting
for? Get up and do something about your life!

E+R=O. I'll say it again, just in case you missed it the
first three times I mentioned it, E+R=O. Sitting back
and watching, hoping and dreaming won't cut it – get off
your tired, frightened-of-failure ass and get moving.

One of the best motivational speakers I have heard in
recent times was Pete Goss. Pete has a truly remarkable
story. If you get a chance to read his book or hear him
speak, I would strongly recommend you do. His book,

> Do the thing and you will have the power.
> – *Ralph Waldo Emerson*

Close to the Wind, details one of the most incredible adventures ever recorded and is an excellent example of how action creates positive change – even when you don't plan for it. Pete had a goal: to sail and compete in the Vendee Global challenge. He made it his goal and gave everything he had to achieving his dream. He made it.

Most people will tell you to focus on the finishing line and not let obstacles get in your way. Whilst this is true, sometimes things happen that are so compelling that you have to do what is in your heart and ignore your plans. Pete did exactly that when he changed course to rescue a fellow competitor. He saved his life – without a doubt – but his decision meant that he had to sacrifice his dream of crossing the finishing line. His decision was brave, not just because of the very real danger he faced in making his rescue attempt, but because it takes a strong heart to let go of a dream – even in the face of a life or death situation. The IMPACT Pete had, not only on Raphael Dinelli, deserves much more than just the MBE he was awarded. Pete would probably tell you that he did indeed get much more from the experience than you could ever imagine.

It takes a brave man to tread another path and take the
road less travelled. Do you think Pete Goss regrets not
finishing the race? I didn't ask if he might have been a
bit disappointed not to have finished the race, I asked if
he regretted it. No way, not for a second. His decision to
let go, change course and try to save the life of his fellow
competitor changed both of their lives forever. He made
it to the real finishing line. His life was enough, he was
enough. Crossing the finishing line of the race wasn't
important enough to let go of the real prize – Pete Goss.
He was his own reward and the amazing life he leads is
everything he could have hoped for in return for his out-
standing effort and determination to achieve his dreams.

Ask yourself honestly if there isn't one thing – no matter
how small – you could do today, right now, to take you
a step closer to your dream. You can't do it all in one day,
but you can do one thing today that will make a positive
IMPACT. It doesn't matter how radical your plans are,
when you break your plan down into bite-size pieces you
can make a start right away. There's still time for the kids,
the shopping and work, just as there is always time for
you and your dreams.

In a nation of millions and a world of billions, the individual
is still the first and basic agent of change. – *Lyndon B. Johnson*

Get ready for action

Do you make the most of every opportunity that comes your way? Probably not. Whenever I present my IMPACT Code I stop part way through the presentation, get a £20 note out of my pocket, hold it up and ask if anyone wants the money. You'd think it would be a no-brainer, wouldn't you? I mean, who would say no to £20? I have played this game all around the world and the outcome is always the same. Silence, followed by a little more silence, followed by giggles. I even hear people telling their colleagues to go up and get the money. Which is bizarre...get someone else to take the risk and reap the rewards...huh?

EVENTUALLY, and usually in a burst of frantic energy, somebody runs up to the stage and grabs the money out of my hand. At which point everyone claps and the lucky winner immediately tries to give the money back! Even though I offered it to them, with no strings attached, people find it impossible to take advantage of the opportunity. It could be that people are too polite and feel uncomfortable taking money off a stranger. I doubt it, by that point in my presentations every barrier has been broken down and the atmosphere is very relaxed. No, there is only one reason why I am never mobbed on stage for my £20.

Hundreds of internal Commentators are shouting commands into the ears of the audience. 'IT'S AN EVIL TRICK! IF YOU RUN UP THERE TO COLLECT THE MONEY EVERYONE WILL LAUGH, YOU DON'T UNDERSTAND THE GAME, IT CAN'T BE THAT SIMPLE, YOU'RE GOING TO MAKE A FOOL OF YOURSELF AND YES…YOUR BUM DOES LOOK BIG IN THAT!'

The key reasons why people don't come up for the money are ego and emotion. If you take the 'e' off both words what do you get? Go and Motion!

About three years ago I was standing on stage holding my £20 and taking in the silence. In the corner of the room a young woman was sitting all alone and she had kept her face turned away from me during the entire speech. Suddenly she sprang into action, she literally leapt across tables and chairs and launched herself at the stage (the

Treasure this day, and treasure yourself. Truly, neither will
ever happen again. – *Ray Bradbury*

video is hilarious – lots of chairs crashing and footage of me silently mouthing several expletives…I thought my number was up). She grabbed the money out of my hand and triumphantly raised up her hands – she was ecstatic. When I looked again I saw she had a very large birth mark on her face, but she was holding her head up and smiling. I asked her what had prompted such an emotional response and she looked me straight in the eye and said, 'I've listened to what you have been saying, I've heard what you said and I just decided that I was never going to let my face get in the way of me taking action ever again.'

She got the biggest round of applause I have ever heard and her extraordinary courage has stayed with me for years. That's what taking action is all about; that's what 'putting your life right' really means.

'Every day is an opportunity to change things for the better.'

– *Michael Pivec*

Your goal is to be in the room and make the most of every moment. If you allow your internal commentator to hold you back you won't be able to move forward. You have to learn to work within the frame of E+R=O.

Thinking about IMPACT, and what it could mean to your life, will give you the impetus to step up to the challenges and take affirmative action. Thinking, dreaming, planning and sharing are all good, but without action it's just procrastination.

Don't just talk about it, do it!

Remember this game?

Connect all of the dots with straight lines without taking your pen off the paper and going back over the same line

Normal is not something to aspire to, it's something to get away from. – *Jodie Foster*

twice. Complete the nine dot puzzle with no more than four lines and the sixteen dot version with no more than six straight lines.

I mention it again just in case you didn't do it the first time, or maybe you did it, but cheated. Why not have another go without cheating? Keep doing it until you get it right. You know where the answers are if you really can't face having a go on your own.

How long can you be in the room with yourself? How long would you allow yourself to take action, seeing it through, making mistakes or getting it right? How long do you give yourself to get your life right? Not long enough, I fear.

You see, whilst I agree that planning and preparation are very important, at some point you have to make a start. Will you mess up, get it wrong, not make the impact you wanted? Possibly, but doing nothing never changed the world. For every Action there is feedback or, as I like to think of it, feedforward. I've already said it once, but it deserves a second airing. The universe always rewards action not thought.

Here's the thing. Before you take action you have to sort out your commitment issues. I'm not talking about your commitment to your job or your kids; I am talking about your commitment to yourself. Love yourself enough to make some real commitments to you. Agree with yourself that even though you may have to compromise along the way, and you may stray from the path you have chosen today, you are going to commit to taking positive action, you are going to commit to change.

'Until one is committed there is hesitancy, the chance to draw back, always ineffectiveness. Concerning all aspects of initiative and creation there is one elementary truth, the ignorance of which kills countless ideas and splendid plans, that the moment one definitely commits oneself then providence moves too. All sorts of things occur to

If we always do what we always did, we will always get what
we always got. – *Jackie 'Moms' Mabley*

help one that would otherwise not have occurred,
a whole stream of events issue from the decision,
raising in one's favour all manner of unforeseen
incidents and meetings plus material assistance
which no man could have dreamed would have
come this way. Whatever you can do, or dream you
can do, begin it. Boldness has genius, power and
magic in it. Begin it now.'

— *Johann Wolfgang Goethe*

Light a candle or two

There is an old saying that it is 'better to light a single candle, than to curse the darkness'. Never is that more true than in achieving your goals and creating impact. Every day, people tell me about things they wish were different. Sometimes they tell me about 'big things' like creating the career or family of their dreams. And sometimes, they talk about the details, 'I wish I could lose 5lbs for the holidays.'

What I have observed, with utter amazement over the years, is how often we all choose to curse in darkness rather than take even one small, useful action. One of the most common techniques for cursing the darkness is to rationalize that our biggest dreams will take too long. Some people complain that it will take years of college to get their degree. Others claim that they will start saving for retirement 'later'. This week, one person told me there was no point in saving for a home of her own because, 'it would take me five years to save that much!'

Change starts when someone sees the next step.
– *William Drayton*

'The greater danger for most of us is not that our
aim is too high and we miss it. But that it is too
low…and we reach it.'

Michelangelo 1475–1564

If you have already done some work on thinking about
your passion and how you want to change your life,
chances are you are a little bit freaked out right now; so
much to do, not enough of you to go around? Knowing
where to start is the hardest part, so break it down and
work on your goal one tiny step at a time. Today's goal
might be just to tell your partner what you have always
dreamed about and ask for their input about how you can
achieve your goals. Nothing will excite you more than the
energy you get from others when you share your 'dirty
little secret' with them.

People really do want to help and you will be surprised
how constructive others can be. Your family may try to
warn you off taking a risk. Don't dismiss them immediately. Think about what they have said and why. Chances
are that their intentions are not sinister; they just don't
want you to be disappointed if you don't achieve your
aim.

That said, if they hold you back and turn into psychic vampires then you have to learn how to 'tune' them out of your conscious brain or get them out of your life. Don't allow their voices to add to the power of your internal commentator. However, my experience is that your loved ones are more likely to find ways to help you rather than hold you back.

'If you hear a voice within saying, "you can't paint," then by all means paint and that voice will be silenced.'

— Vincent van Gogh

When you start taking action, your family will understand why and will support you. If you have already shared that there are aspects of your life that you don't like, but tell them that you know that you have to keep doing it, they will help you in your efforts to do the things you do like. Without the support of my family I would not have been able to get as far along my career path as I have. When I walked away from my business to pursue other things, I put my family in harm's way financially. For a brief moment I was crippled by what I had

We're all working together; that's the secret. – *Sam Walton, founder of the Wal-Mart empire*

done, but with my wife's support I realized that in fact I was working for them as well as myself.

She made me see that the risk I had taken was worth every moment of financial strife. Together we made it work and it has paid off for us. I firmly believe that the only reason she was able to help me through it was because she knew what I wanted in the long term, where I saw myself going and how I saw my family fitting in to that. She knew that my dreams were as much about her as they were about me – it made it easier for both of us to cope with the upheaval.

Your dreams may not involve your family – your dreams may even take you away from your family. Whatever your heart desires is what you should aim for. If you are unhappy, do something about it, get a plan in place and start making the small moves that will lead to your bigger dream.

Small action, big change

One stormy night many years ago, an elderly man and his
wife entered the lobby of a small hotel in Philadelphia.
Trying to get out of the rain, the couple approached the
front desk hoping to get some shelter for the night.

'Could you possibly give us a room here?' the husband
asked. The clerk, a friendly man with a winning smile,
looked at the couple and explained that there were three
conventions in town.

'All of our rooms are taken,' the clerk said. 'But I can't
send a nice couple like yourselves out in the rain at one
o'clock in the morning. Would you perhaps be willing
to sleep in my room? It's not exactly a suite, but it will
be good enough to make you folks comfortable for the
night.' When the couple declined, the young man pressed
on. 'Don't worry about me. I'll be just fine,' he told them.
So the couple agreed.

As long as I have to die my own death, I have decided to live
my own life and not let others live it for me.
– *Hanoch McCarthy*

As he paid the bill the next morning, the elderly man said
to the clerk, 'You are the kind of manager who should
be the boss of the best hotel in the United States. Maybe
someday I'll build one for you.'

The clerk looked at the couple and smiled. The three of
them had a good laugh together. As they drove away, the
elderly couple agreed that the helpful clerk was indeed
exceptional, and pondered on the fact that finding people
who are both friendly and helpful isn't easy.

Two years passed. The clerk had almost forgotten the
incident when he received a letter from the old man.
It recalled that stormy night and enclosed a round-trip
ticket to New York, asking the young man to pay them a
visit. The old man met him in New York, and led him to
the corner of Fifth Avenue and 34th Street.

He then pointed to a great new building there, a palace of
reddish stone, with turrets and watchtowers thrusting up
to the sky.

'That,' said the older man, 'is the hotel I have just built
for you to manage.'

'You must be joking!' the young man said.

'I can assure you that I am not!' said the older man, a sly smile playing around his mouth.

The old man's name was William Waldorf Astor, and the magnificent structure was the original Waldorf-Astoria Hotel. The young clerk who became its first manager was George C Bokit. This young clerk never foresaw the turn of events that would lead him to become the manager of one of the world's most glamorous hotels.

They say never turn your back on those who are in need – for you may be entertaining angels! Creating IMPACT, helping others and ultimately helping ourselves can only lead you forward, never back.

'If you want a thing bad enough to go out and fight for it, to work day and night for it, to give up your time, your peace and your sleep for it…if all that you dream and scheme is about it, and life seems useless and worthless without it…if you gladly sweat for it and fret for it and plan for it and lose all your terror of the opposition for it…if you simply go

Standing your ground is progress when you are
battling a hurricane. – *Franklin Lane*

after that thing you want with all of your capacity,
strength and sagacity, faith, hope and confidence
and stern pertinacity…if neither cold, poverty,
famine, nor gout, sickness nor pain, of body and
brain, can keep you away from the thing that you
want…if dogged and grim you beseech and beset it,
with the help of God, you WILL get it!'

– Berton Bradly

Start with yourself

The following words were written on the tomb of an
Anglican Bishop in the Crypts of Westminster Abbey.

'When I was young and free and my imagination
had no limits, I dreamed of changing the world. As
I grew older and wiser, I discovered the world would
not change, so I shortened my sights somewhat
and decided to change only my country. But it too
seemed immovable. As I grew into my twilight
years, in one last desperate attempt, I settled for
changing only my family, those closest to me, but
alas, they would have none of it. And now, as I lie
on my deathbed, I suddenly realize: If I had only
changed my self first, then by example I would have
changed my family. From their inspiration and
encouragement, I would then have been able to
better my country and who knows, I may have even
changed the world.'

One person with courage makes a majority.
– *Andrew Jackson*

You can't aim a duck to death

Every morning in Africa, a gazelle wakes up. It knows it must run faster than the fastest lion or it will be killed. Every morning a lion wakes up and it knows it must out-run the slowest gazelle or it will starve to death. You see, it does not matter whether you are a lion or a gazelle; when the sun comes up you had better be running.

'Knowledge is power' is probably the most damning (and irritating) statement I've ever heard. I am pretty certain that both the lion and the gazelle know the score when the sun comes up. You see, you have to take action in order to get your goal or ensure that your dreams are met.

Just thinking about it won't work. So, I guess we have to rewrite that old favourite: 'Knowledge, with action, is power.'

Far-off shores

We all spend far too much time on 'Someday Isle'. Let's
face it; Someday Isle is the island of choice for just about
every adult around the world. You can do so much when
you get there – it's incredible.

Someday Isle…write a book
Someday Isle…leave my job
Someday Isle…ask for a pay rise

I want you to be aware that Action without Purpose or
Passion is a nightmare and Purpose without Action is a
daydream.

'You only live once, but if you work it right, once is
enough.'

— *Joe E. Lewis*

Do not wait for life. Be aware at every moment that the
miracle is in the here and now. – *Marcel Proust*

Sense and sensibility

A US businessman was at the pier of a small coastal Mexican fishing village when a small boat with just one fisherman docked. Inside the boat were several large yellow-fin tuna. The American complimented the Mexican on the quality of his fish and asked how long it took to catch them.

The Mexican replied, 'Only a little while, señor.' The American asked why he didn't stay out longer and catch more fish. The Mexican said that he had enough to supply his family's immediate needs.

The American then asked, 'But what do you do with the rest of your time?'

The fisherman said, 'I play with my children, take siesta with my wife, Maria, stroll into the village each evening where I sip wine and play guitar with my amigos. I have a full and busy life, señor.'

The American smiled, 'I have a Harvard MBA – that's a degree in business studies – I could help you. You should spend more time fishing and with the proceeds buy a bigger boat, with the proceeds from the bigger boat you could buy several boats, eventually you would have a fleet. Then instead of selling your catch to a middleman you would sell directly to the processor, eventually opening your own cannery. You would control the product, processing and distribution. You would, of course, need to leave this small coastal fishing village and move to Mexico City, then Los Angeles and eventually New York City where you would run your expanding enterprise.'

The Mexican fisherman asked, 'But, señor, how long would all this take?'

The American replied, 'Fifteen to twenty years.'

'But what then, señor?'

The American laughed, 'That's the best part. When the time is right you sell your stock to the public and become very rich. You would make millions.'

Most of the things worth doing in the world were said to be
impossible before they were done. – *Louis D Brandeis*

'Millions, señor? But then what?'

'Then you would retire, move to a small coastal fishing village, where you could sleep late, fish a little, play with your kids, take siesta with your wife, Maria, and stroll to the village in the evenings where you could sip wine and play your guitar with your amigos.'

With just the hint of a twinkle in his eye, the fisherman said, 'Señor – are these business degrees hard to get?'

You need to take exactly the right amount of action to get what you want. When you have what you want, you need to take exactly the right amount of action to keep your dream alive.

Exercise

Answer the following questions and start to identify your goal. Then commit to achieving it, break it down into a series of smaller goals and get started.

- In what areas do I want to make an IMPACT?
- What are the benefits of achieving this?
- What fears, considerations and roadblocks may I encounter?
- What skills or coaching will be required to create an IMPACT?
- What is my plan of Action to start the process?
- When do I want to do this by?

Let go of something you hate doing; do something brave today. Ring that awful client; speak to a friend or relative you have been avoiding. Make a list of people who bother you and why, task yourself with ousting at least one relationship demon a day for the next week and see how different you feel when you are done.

Obstacles don't make people stop – people stop themselves.
– *Carol Quinn*

CHAPTER FIVE

The ImpaCt Code

C = Comic relief

If you're not having fun, why are you doing it?

Comic relief – summary

Factor some fun into every day.

The fastest way to super-charge your success is to find the lighter side in every situation and share it with the world.

Don't take yourself too seriously – you might find you're the only one not laughing if you do!

Smile and the world WILL smile with you.

No matter what crap life throws your way, don't take it too seriously. Life goes on regardless, there's no sense wasting time being angry or sad about it.

Being smart does not have to mean being grumpy. Let the world see the intellect hiding behind your smile.

Forgive yourself first and then forgive the world.

Comic relief

'One can discover more about a person in an hour
of play than in a year of conversation.'

– Plato

If I were to watch you for an hour while you play or have
fun, what would I say about you when the hour was
up? The older we get the less we seem to laugh. Is life so
crappy that there isn't anything to laugh about any more
or is it that we have got lost in the drama of it all?

The further along the road of life we go, the more com-
plicated it all seems to get. Work pressures, family responsibilities, exhaustion, frustration, so the list goes on. It's
easy to fall into the habit of being too serious. When we
were kids our parents would constantly remind us that
when we 'grew up' we would have to be serious and not
be silly anymore. God knows why! Life is hard enough
without being a total bore about the whole thing. Without laughter we are surely beaten.

Believe in something big, your life deserves a noble motive.
– Walter Anderson

It is a medical fact that laughter is good for the body as well as the soul. But nothing will aid creating IMPACT more than laughter, good humour and a sincere smile. It's pretty obvious stuff but think about the people in your life. Who would you rather help or work with? A serious-minded grump or a light-hearted, forgiving ally?

There isn't a single thing that happens – not one – that can't be taken with a light heart. We have all had our share of misfortune and tragedy. Life is hard, life can be cruel, but as I have said before, we choose how to deal with life, not the other way around. So, it's up to you; smile and get what you want or frown and wait a lifetime for not a great deal to happen to you.

E+R=O

Some of the funniest people I know have some of the most responsible jobs on the planet. Surgeons are a particularly witty bunch. Imagine if they took themselves too seriously. The emotional burden of what they do every day of their working lives would be too much to bear without a wry smile and a wink in the face of adversity.

Surgeons are the ultimate team players; they work in a highly charged stressful environment, with a tightly knit group of highly skilled professionals. Lives are at stake, so it is important that every member of the team is comfortable enough to do their best. The last thing the surgeon, or the patient, wants is for everyone in the theatre to be worrying about the mood of the surgeon or living up to his or her high standards. What the surgeon and patient want is for everyone to be worrying about what they do best – caring for the patient. They all need to be in the room!

Taking a light-hearted approach to life and work is the surest way to earn the respect of those around you. If you can smile in the face of adversity and forgive when others tell you that you shouldn't, then the world will be your oyster. In every facet of our daily lives we can find something to smile about. It's there; you just have to WANT to find it.

Remember the first rule of modelling – 'fake it till you make it'. If you don't feel like smiling, do it anyway. It really will make you feel better. Your family, friends and work colleagues will work harder to help you when you

The world is your world. Take it easy, but take it.
– *Woody Guthrie*

smile than when you frown. If you doubt that just keep asking yourself if you would want to work with you today.

Tragedy and heartbreak are a fact of life. The natural balance of the universe seems to preclude the possibility of things being good all of the time. There are so many horrific things happening around the world, there are days when it is tough to find anything good to smile about. Here's the thing. You won't change anything if you don't change yourself first. Comic relief is probably the one area of the IMPACT code that enables you to positively affect the world around you with very little effort.

We can all help raise funds for the stricken or feel sorry for the victims of crime, but other than that there is very little we can do as individuals to help. Well, yes and no. Imagine a world where everyone smiled. Imagine a place where important tasks and difficult problems were tackled light-heartedly rather than with a frown and a side order of stress. How much tension would be relieved around the world if we all took life just a little bit less seriously? You can't change the world in a day, but you can start today – with a smile.

Smiles are more contagious than the flu. Good humour breeds loyalty, love and community. In an atmosphere of happiness, stress dissipates to nothing, mistakes become lessons learned and disasters are just something to work through rather than complete 'road blocks'.

The ripple effect of the IMPACT code starts here. When you have focused on your dreams and decided what you want to achieve for yourself, be happy. You are starting on a journey that will make your life richer and you should be damn happy about it – otherwise what the hell are you doing it for?

You can still have fun while you are doing something you don't want to do, or don't particularly enjoy. Just getting through a task that will either help your family or take you a step closer to your dream should be enough to keep you smiling. If the job in hand is truly boring then make it your business to make it fun for you and everyone you work with. Time really does fly when you are having fun.

I guarantee you that there isn't a single person on this earth who doesn't find at least one aspect of their life dull. Housework sucks, but I prefer to live in a clean house, so

You're only given a little spark of madness.
You mustn't lose it. – *Robin Williams*

to get through it I play loud music while I work. Reliving my youth while I clean the bath tub makes the time fly. I just want to point out (before my wife murders me) I don't do it very often, but when I do I try not to moan about it and try to make the best of it.

A good friend of mine used to run a marketing agency and occasionally she would be forced to accept an unrealistic client deadline which meant that her team had to come in to work on the weekend and stuff envelopes to get a mail shot out in time. On one such weekend, eight people volunteered to help and they had 35,000 envelopes to stuff. So, rather than just going at it in one sitting, she devised a series of games and activities to keep everyone awake and break up the time (and take their minds off the boredom). She decorated the office as if they were having a kid's birthday party, ordered a ton of great party food and played music all day. She arranged transportation to and from the office and put everyone up in a hotel on the Saturday night. The wine flowed, the laughter followed and by the middle of the second day the job was done, the team was set and the client was very happy. Everyone came into work on Monday with a spring in their step.

Imagine how different that weekend would have been if
she had just produced thousands of flyers and envelopes
and made no effort to help everyone get through the or-
deal. They probably would have still got the job done, but
Monday morning would have been a very different experience for everyone. With a little effort and a big heart
you can achieve so much more than you can by being too
serious. I am not saying that you shouldn't afford a situation or challenge the proper amount of respect, but you
don't have to be a grouch about it. There's enough stress
in our lives without adding our weight behind it.

My rule in life is simple. The more important the job, the
more difficult the challenge, the bigger my smile has to
be. It works.

I have done a considerable amount of work with Red Bull
over the last couple of years and what distinguishes this
drinks company from the others is the way it has aligned
itself to not only extreme sports, but to comic ways of
going to the extreme.

For example, every year Red Bull sponsors a competition
to see who can fly the furthest when jumping off a bridge

Think big thoughts, but relish small pleasures.
– *Jackson Brown, Jr.*

without using anything electrical. Totally insane, incredibly funny and good fun for everyone involved. But it isn't just morale that benefits from the use of humour – since adopting such an edgy, humour-based strategy, sales of Red Bull have gone through the roof. At least we know that Red Bull shareholders are smiling!

Another terrific example of using humour to create a positive working culture is the drinks company Innocent. The company was founded by three young men whilst they were still at university. They made a pact to have fun in every facet of their business. So, when doing market research for their first launch they went to a rock festival, pitched up and took 700 cartons of their 100% fresh juice to see whether there was a market for their product. Everything you need to know about them and their company can be seen in the novel way they went about the task of testing the product.

They placed two large bins next to the table where the samples were laid out, ready for people to dump their empty cartons. Both bins had large labels on the front, one read 'Don't give up your university place' and the other read 'Leave university now'. By the end of the day 699 cartons had been deposited in the 'Leave university now' bin and so they duly gave up their places, set up their business and have never looked back.

The fun did not stop there. Even today, with all of their success, they have stayed true to their belief in the value of fun. Even the packaging speaks volumes about these guys. On each carton of drink, instead of saying 'Use by [DATE]' theirs says 'Enjoy by [DATE]'. They also state that if you ever want to call them call, do it on the Fruit Phone. You may have also seen one of their vehicles...in the shape of a cow!

So you see, your business ethos can include both fun and profit. I would argue that if you crave bigger profits you had better start learning how to laugh. It's up to you to make it work. If we take what Plato had to say about the truth of a man, and apply that to life, what would I learn about your business or family if I watched you and your 'team' for an hour?

Do something. Either lead, follow, or get out of the way.
– *Ted Turner*

When Daniel Brown joined Beaverbrooks Jewellers'
board of directors, one of his tasks was to make sure that
he injected some fun into the organization whilst ensur-
ing customer service never faltered. Daniel is CHO of the
organization, which stands for Chief Humour Officer. If
you are thinking that this would not work for your organization please bear in mind that Beaverbrooks has been
voted the second best company to work for in the Sunday
Times 100 Awards. They care about their people, and in
turn, their people care about their customers. It's a simple
equation that even the most cynical can relate to.

E+R=O

You get what you play for

Now, I hope you realize that I am not suggesting that you go into work tomorrow and start clowning around like an insane circus drop-out. No, fun doesn't start with a whoopee cushion, it starts with not taking yourself too seriously. Say, 'Hi, how are you?' a little more often and make time to stop and hear the reply. Smile when someone makes a hideous mistake and say, 'Never mind, let's fix this together.'

As soon as you start taking yourself too seriously you will instantly become the butt of every joke. When you cut everyone some slack and treat them with respect and good humour they will break their backs to help you achieve your goals – because they know you would do the same for them. The magic of masterminding can apply to your 'informal' team as well as your carefully-constructed Mastermind team. People love happy, reasonable people. Go figure…it's a shocker isn't it?

For things to change, we must change. For things to get better, we must get better. – Heidi Wills

Never was there a better example of how teaching people
how to treat us can pay dividends in our day-to-day lives.
If everywhere you go people seem to be angry and negative or difficult, it is probably because you are. If people
believe that you are unreasonable then they will treat you
that way. How often do people stop and say 'hi' and ask
how you are doing? Maybe you need to shift your attitude
before you ask the same of others. Most people I meet are
great, they smile and laugh and we get through so much
work together. If everyone you meet is closed off and
guarded, I would bet my kids' education that it is because
of the way you treat them and not because they are just
naturally nasty. Almost everyone on this planet is nice
– funny how you only seem to meet the nasty ones.

Then again, you might be a naturally happy person but
you find that this doesn't spill over into to your work, or
you don't make the most of it at work; ask yourself why.
Are you insecure about your talent? Worried that people
will see you as light-weight, rather than light-hearted? Are
you pretending to be serious to earn the respect of those

around you? People probably do like you, but how much more would they like you if they could see the real you? It's no coincidence that most comedians are incredibly intelligent. People see past the smile and admire the intellect behind it.

When you think of Bob Hope do you think 'putz'? When you watch Jim Carrey pulling off a dramatic role do you think 'liar'? No, of course not. Jim Carrey has got talent – by the bucketload – and that is why you can watch him performing serious roles without thinking of him as a fraud and vice versa. He is light-hearted but he is also incredibly successful and very intelligent.

People will see what you want them to see. If you are smart and happy – live that way. Serious does not have to mean grumpy. You can be smart, firm, fair and dedicated without having to be a pain in the ass, who takes yourself and life far too seriously. Get over yourself and start smiling.

Having fun is not a diversion from a successful life; it is the pathway to it. – *Martha Beck*

Look for the good in life and you will find it, look for the good in people and they will show you the good in them and the good in you. Nothing will give your day more meaning than laughter.

Give happiness a go; you never know, you might like it.

E+R=O

Laughter and enthusiasm is contagious – is yours worth catching?

It's a jungle out there

One of the quickest ways to take the potential fun out
of a situation is to 'handle' a person in a way that doesn't
fit with their personality. I find that 95% of people have
one clearly dominant personality trait. The more we
understand about where people (including ourselves) are
coming from, the better we can relate to each other. As
a result, communication becomes more satisfying and
everybody benefits. Over the past ten years I have been
presenting a model of communication which I call 'zoo
keeping'. It places people into four broad personality
types: monkey, lion, elephant and dolphin.

To be an effective zoo keeper, you need to understand
each style: your own, and those of the people with whom
you work. This will give you a greater insight into the
individuals who make up your 'team'. As you recognize
what makes each person special and find ways to tap into
the group's diversity, your team will grow stronger. When
individuals are encouraged to work to their strengths, it
brings out the best in everyone.

If you're not enjoying the journey, you probably
won't enjoy the destination. – *Joe Tye*

Know your animals

One of your most valuable skills as a zoo keeper is your
ability to understand your animals. They are constantly
sending you signals about their needs and feelings. When
you can interpret these correctly you'll know how to work
with them most effectively. So what is there to know?

Human animals have many subtle ways of communicating. You can pick up their signals if all your senses are
tuned in. When you are aware of the visual, aural, kin-
esthetic, emotional and other sensory cues that they are
transmitting, you will know how to relate to them. You'll
know when to speed up or slow down, when to focus on
the details, or when to work on backing off from a relationship with the other person.

We all have the same basic human needs, but you may
measure success differently from the way I do.

Some people measure success by results. They'll work
their hearts out to get the job done. They are prepared

to sacrifice a great deal to achieve the finished product because that's how they measure success. They need to accomplish something tangible. Other people gauge success in terms of their relationships. These individuals are typically sensitive, warm and supportive. They will work well if they feel that they and their colleagues are valued. They put people before results. Then there are those who measure their success in terms of the recognition they receive. They need to know that others think highly of them and their work. Acknowledgement and praise are very important to them. Finally, there are the people who are more concerned with the content than the congratulations. They like things to be well structured and organized and clearly understood. They measure success by the quality of the work they produce. Usually, they are able to measure the quality themselves – they don't need anyone else to tell them when they've done a good job.

The skillful zoo keeper recognizes that each of these four types will respond to different strategies. Once you realize this you can work out how best to communicate with a wide variety of people.

> Enjoy yourself. These are the 'good old days' you're going to
> miss years ahead. We can never go back again,
> that much is certain. – *B. J. Marshall*

Who's grooming who?

I have written a separate book about 'zoo keeping' which goes into detail about how to work and live with every type of 'animal' you are going to encounter, but for now here is a quick summary of each animal type. Hopefully, this will help you interact and pick the fleas off your next encounter. If you want to know more about how to deal with each animal type, then you can pick up *It's a zoo around here* from my website (details at the back of the book).

The Monkey

Open and direct.

The monkey has high levels of both directness and openness. Monkeys are animated, intuitive and lively. They are ideas people, and can get very enthusiastic about their plans. However, others may see them as manipulative.

Monkeys are fast-paced people who act and make decisions spontaneously. They are not concerned about facts and details, and try to avoid them as much as possible. This disregard for details may prompt them at times to exaggerate and generalize facts and figures.

Monkeys are more comfortable with 'best guesstimates' than with carefully researched facts. They thrive on involvement with people and usually work quickly and enthusiastically with others.

Monkeys always seem to be chasing dreams. They are so persuasive that others can easily get caught up in their dreams. Monkeys always seem to be seeking approval and pats on the back for their accomplishments and achievements. They are socializers: creative, dynamic and able to think on their feet.

Dominant characteristics of the monkey:
• Has plenty of ideas
• Knows how to have fun
• Enjoys a joke
• Is very creative

Imagination continually frustrates tradition. That's its job.
– *John Pfeiffer*

- Likes examples and pictures
- Gets bored easily.

How to address monkeys:
- Ask them for ideas
- Be energetic
- Make it fun.

Communicating negative feedback:
- Talk to the monkey in private
- Be prepared to argue.

Use the 'sandwich' technique as a cushioning device:
- Build them up (the first banana)
- Give them the feedback (the nut)
- Build them up again (the second banana).

The Lion

Direct and guarded.

Lions are very direct and, at the same time, guarded. They exhibit firmness in their relationships with others, are oriented towards productivity and goals, and are concerned with bottom-line results. Closely allied to these positive traits, however, are some negative ones: the lion can be stubborn, impatient, tough and even domineering.

Lions tend to take control of other people and situations and be decisive in both their actions and decisions. They like to move at an extremely fast pace and are very impatient with delays. When other people can't keep up with their speed, they view them as incompetent. The lion's motto might well be, 'I want it done right and I want it done now.'

Lions are typically high achievers who exhibit very good administrative skills; they certainly get things done and make things happen. Lions like to do many things at the same time. They may start by juggling three things at the same time, and as soon as they feel comfortable with those they pick up a fourth. They keep adding on until the pressure builds to such a point that they turn their backs and let everything drop. Then they turn right around and start the whole process all over again.

Dominant characteristics of the lion:
• Task/results-oriented

Live your life as an exclamation rather than an explanation.
 – *Bob Newton*

- Efficient and effective
- Likes to be in charge.

How to address lions:
- Don't waste time
- Be brief and to the point
- Speak directly
- Spell out the bottom line.

Communicating negative feedback:
- Avoid doing this in public
- Be brief and to the point
- The lion will get over it and keep on functioning.

The Elephant

Indirect and guarded.

People who have elephant characteristics are both indirect and guarded. They seem to be very concerned with the process of thinking and are persistent, systematic problem-solvers. However, they also can be seen as aloof, picky and critical. Elephants are very security-conscious and have a strong need to be right. This leads them to an over-reliance on data collection. In their quest for data they tend to ask lots of questions about specific details. This can be infuriating to monkeys and lions.

Elephants' actions and decisions tend to be extremely cautious. They tend to work slowly and precisely by themselves and prefer an intellectual work environment that is organized and structured. They tend to be sceptical and like to see things in writing. Although they are great problem-solvers, elephants are poor decision-makers. They may keep collecting data even beyond the time when a decision is due, justifying their caution by saying, 'When you are making vast decisions, you cannot do it on half-vast data.'

Dominant characteristics of the elephant:
• Collects information
• Needs accurate details
• Likes to analyse things
• Sensitive
• Vulnerable.

How to address elephants:
• Talk quietly and gently

Changing one small thing for the better is worth more than
proving a thousand people wrong. – *Anthony Pivec*

- Go into detail.

Communicating negative feedback:
- This must be done in private.
- After giving the feedback, outline two or three steps
  that the elephant can take to rectify any problems.

The Dolphin

Open and indirect.

The fourth and last style, the dolphin, is open and unas-
sertive, warm, supportive and reliable. However, the
dolphin sometimes is seen by others as compliant, soft-
hearted and acquiescent. Dolphins seek security and like
to feel that they belong. Like the elephant, the dolphin is
slow at taking action and making decisions. This procrastination stems from a desire to avoid risky and unknown
situations. Before dolphins take action or make decisions,
they have to know how other people feel.

The dolphin is the most people-oriented of all four styles.
Having close, friendly, personal and first-name relation-

ships with others is one of the most important objectives
of the dolphin's style.

Dolphins dislike interpersonal conflicts so much that
they sometimes say what they think other people want to
hear rather than what they really think. Dolphins have
tremendous counselling skills and are extremely supportive of other people. They are also incredibly active
listeners. You usually feel good just being with a dolphin.
Because dolphins listen so well to other people, when it
is their turn to talk, people usually listen. This gives them
an excellent ability to gain support from others.

Dominant characteristics of the dolphin:
• Sensitive
• Tuned in to people's emotions
• Vulnerable
• Interested in details.

How to address dolphins:
• Use a quiet tone of voice
• Be gentle
• Be prepared to go into detail.

Remember when you were at your best? Now be there again!
– *Andrew Mead*

Communicating negative feedback:
• Say 'we' and 'us', even if you need to fire the dolphin
• Be fair.

Zoo keeping for beginners

For now, all you need to understand is that everyone is dominated by a strong personality type, which I have likened to animal types. We're all a bit of everything, but one animal always leads. Keeping the fun in your life means that you must strive to understand people; what makes them tick, laugh and spit! Look around you and consider who is in your life. Think about which relationships are working and which aren't. Then ask yourself what type of person is involved in each relationship and how much their dominant personality type affects your ability to interact with them. You might be surprised at what you find. Good hunting!

Something to smile about

If you are feeling a bit low, here are a few things to make you smile. These are all taken from actual advertisements, signs or notices. You see, even we can take a break from changing the universe for ten minutes to have a bit of fun!

- Lost: small apricot poodle. Reward. Neutered. Like one of the family.
- Dinner Special – Turkey £2.35; Chicken or Beef £2.25; Children £2.00.
- For sale – an antique desk suitable for lady with thick legs and large drawers.
- Now is your chance to have your ears pierced and get an extra pair to take home too.
- For sale – eight puppies from a German Shepherd and an Alaskan Hussy.
- Great Dames for sale.
- If you think you've seen everything in Paris, visit the Pere Lachasis Cemetery. It boasts such immortals as Moliere and Chopin.

Live out of your imagination instead of out of your memory.
– *Les Brown*

- Stock up and save. Limit: one.
- Used cars: why go elsewhere to be cheated? Come here first!
- Modular sofas. Only £299. For rest or fore play.
- Our experienced mum will care for your child. Fenced yard, meals, and smacks included.
- Our bikinis are exciting. They are simply the tops.
- Auto Repair Service. Free pick-up and delivery. Try us once, you'll never go anywhere else again.
- Wanted: Preparer of food. Must be dependable, like the food business, and be willing to get hands dirty.
- Girl wanted to assist magician in cutting-off-head illusion. BUPA and salary.
- Mother's helper – peasant working conditions.
- Semi-Annual after-Christmas Sale.
- And now, the Superstore – unequalled in size, unmatched in variety, unrivalled inconvenience.

The Risk Poem

To laugh is to risk appearing a fool,
To cry is to risk appearing sentimental and soft,
To reach out to another is to risk involvement,
To show up and expose your feelings is to risk
exposing your inherent self,
To place your ideas, your dreams, your desires before
people is to risk their loss,
To love is to risk not being loved in return,
To show strength is to risk showing weakness,
To do is to risk failure.
The greatest hazard in life is to risk nothing,
The person who risks nothing gets nothing, has
nothing, is nothing.
He may avoid suffering, pain, sorrow, but he does
not live, he does not love,
He has sold, forfeited freedom, integrity,
He is a slave, chained by safety, locked away by fear.
Because, only a person who is willing to risk not
knowing the result is FREE.

— Anonymous

Quality begins with character. *— Amos Laurence*

A friend in need

Margaret was at work when she got a call that her daughter was very sick at school. She stopped by the pharmacy to get some medication. When returning to her car she found that she had locked her keys in the car. Looking around in desperation she found an old rusty coat hanger thrown down possibly by someone else who had locked their keys in their car.

A man got out of his nearby car and asked her if he could help. She said, 'Yes, my daughter is very sick … I stopped to get her some medication and I've locked by keys in my car, I must get home to her.' He said, 'Sure,' and walked over to the car. In less than one minute the car was opened.

She hugged him and through her tears she said, 'THANK YOU SO MUCH. You are a very nice man.' The man replied, 'Lady, I am not a nice man. I was in prison for car theft and have only been out for about an hour.'

She hugged the man again and with tears in her eyes she cried out loud … 'THANK YOU, LORD, FOR SENDING ME A PROFESSIONAL.'

Exercise

Think back to the last time you were really cheesed off about something. Think about it for a minute. Now think about it from the point of view of finding the lighter side to the situation. Notice how much tension is relieved when you look at it with different eyes.

Watch a funny film. Go dancing or do something completely pointless that just makes your heart soar (don't worry about being the oldest groover in town, just let your hair down and go for it). NOTHING will recharge your batteries quite like pointless fun.

There will come a time when you believe everything is finished. That will be the beginning. – *Louis L'Amour*

CHAPTER SIX

The Impac T Code

T = Trust

Without trust, you're finished before you start

Trust – summary

Trust yourself. Trust your gut.

Trust your team. Mastermind your success.

Trust your God. Have faith in the world, have faith in yourself.

Learn to trust.

We all have achieved success in the past; write down your success, think back to past success. Keep telling yourself you 'can' by reminding yourself that you 'have already'. You can do it.

Your team is the best asset you have; when you are surrounded by the right people you will be amazed at what you can achieve.

Trust your 'God' – there is something called faith.

Trust your 'God', whatever form your faith takes…

Trust

For most people, this is one of the most difficult aspects of creating IMPACT. Our cynical adult minds make it difficult to trust people. It's a shame. We tell kids off for trusting people too quickly; we worry constantly about where misplaced trust will take them. We bang 'stranger danger' into their heads day and night and wonder why they grow up bitter and angry. The statistics about 'stranger danger' are clear…there virtually isn't a danger, so why do we frighten them with it? Our kids are more at risk from obesity and diabetes then they are from abduction and murder (by a long, long way). But we impose our fears and mistrust on them. It taints them, but we do it from a place of love so it is hard not to do it. The same is true of trusting in other aspects of our lives. We want to do the right thing, but it is really tough to let go and be vulnerable. We are all afraid of being let down.

Trust, or the lack of it, has much to do with what is wrong in the world today. As the years march by, society

Remember that you are unique, and if that is not fulfilled,
then something has been lost. – *Martha Graham*

is becoming more fragmented and individuals are losing touch with their respective communities. The less contact we have with the 'outside' world the more likely we are to fall victim to trust issues. If you suffer at the hands of a wicked person then it is easy to see how you could fall into the trap of assuming everyone is untrustworthy. Getting back to how the brain works, your head will 'tell' you, very clearly, that avoiding people is the surest way to avoid danger. It is true, that if we allow other people into our lives we are exposing ourselves to risk.

So, why risk it? It's simple really. A life without other people isn't much of a life at all. Not only do we need others to help us achieve our dreams, we need other people to breathe, live and develop. Not every experience will be a good one. Nobody can protect you from bad people, but even bad experiences can lead you to a more positive outcome and better relationships with the remaining people in your life. Without trust we cease to be compassionate and we lose grip of what makes us human. It is our vulnerability that makes us what we are. We need others and the process of handing ourselves over to their care can be terrifying.

Some people trust without a second thought and are never unsettled when they get let down. Are they simply naive or are they in fact the ultimate realists?

Trusting others can be uncomfortable, particularly when the person you trust least is yourself. It has been my experience that the people who shout loudest about not trusting anyone else in the world, do in fact have a problem with themselves and not mankind as a whole. If you find it very difficult to trust others, ask yourself why? Is it because you genuinely don't think that person should be trusted or is it because you couldn't trust yourself to do the thing you are asking of them and so why should you trust them with the same task?

If you follow the principles of modelling you need to let go of your inhibitions and accept that we all need to trust in order to move forward. Just as you need to love yourself enough to tell the total truth about what you want and go for it, you need to trust yourself to get the job done. When you believe you can do it, you will and you will start to see how much others can do to help you and how much you can help them in return.

I knew someone had to take the first step and I made up my mind not to move. – *Rosa Parks, on her decision to sit in the whites-only section of the bus*

I am not suggesting that you start trusting everyone who crosses your path because not everyone is a good person. What I am saying is that you have to find some kind of balance. Most of us conduct our lives as if every person we encounter is a crook, just waiting for the chance to ruin it all. The truth is that bad people are few and far between. Most people want you to win and can be trusted. We have to let go of our fear without turning off our common sense. You don't have to trust somebody 100% to get along with them but you do need to understand why you don't trust them and be honest with yourself about what drives your mistrust.

For the past two years I have been asked to speak and host a conference for the Northern Housing Consortium. It has always been fun, full of learning and I get a chance to meet some great people who are making a difference.

This year I was asked would it be OK if I had a co-host. When I found out who it was I was delighted. Marie

Mosely is as opposite to me in nearly every way possible.
However, the question I want you to think about is 'Do
you like the people you work with or do you trust them?'
You see, Marie and I have had our differences; she has
given me feedback in the past, some that I have not liked,
but do I trust her? You bet I do. You don't have to like to
trust. Respect and like are not the same thing at all.

I have a Mastermind team I trust 100%. I have a few
friends who I trust 100% (I will not embarrass any of
them, however Harley is a cut above most; he also tells me
what I don't want to hear sometimes). I trust my brother,
my wife and my kids 100%. Who do you trust?

In my opinion if you have a least five people you trust
100% you are doing well. Like I said, it doesn't need to be
100% trust to be effective. Know the limitations of your
trust and don't allow the person you are trusting to step
outside of that zone until they have proven to you that
they are worthy of more. But, be honest about trust and

always check your own answers for misplaced emotional baggage. You might be cutting yourself off from a terrific ally simply because he or she looks like the demon who abused you or sounds like your old head teacher who ridiculed you in public at every opportunity...being 'in the room' with your trust issues is quite an enlightening experience.

A great speaker once said 'it's trust, not like' that makes the world go around.

Judge for yourself

How do you judge people? Does what you believe affect
how you behave?

What are the mechanisms we use to see if we trust
people or not? Our parents – the poor devils are getting
the blame again – have an enormous effect on what we
believe and how we perceive the fabric of the intangible
universe, be that a God or scientific concept in relation
to dealing with life in general. They tell you all kinds of
stupid things and even though logic tells you that they
are wrong you just can't help listening to their voices in
your head. After all, who else can you trust if you can't
trust your parents? The trouble is, being a parent doesn't
automatically qualify you as a wise prophet – you're just
another person doing your best to make your kids' lives
whole.

I mean, remember your first day at work? How many of
us got the same advice about knowing who you could
trust and who you couldn't? Who was fed the line 'you

Excellence is not a spectator sport. Everyone's involved.
– *Jack Welch*

can tell a lot about a person from the firmness of a hand-shake'? As if that makes a difference to anyone or about anything, but think about what you feel when you are greeted by a limp handshake! Something that occurred to me early on about this piece of advice is that it was pretty likely that the crooks knew about this and probably prac-tised their handshakes until they got the grip just right!

I was speaking at an international convention where the protocol is to meet and greet the speaker afterwards; 2,500 people later I could barely move my fingers. Does that make me inferior and non-trusting? Handshakes aside, let's talk about all those people with beards. They've definitely got something to hide.

I spend about a third of my time working with chief executive groups, such as ACE (the Academy of Chief Executives) and Vistage International (originally founded as The Executive Committee). One of my main roles is to bring new groups of CEOs and business leaders together as fast as possible. Picture this scenario.

Every month all over the world, each chapter of ACE bring together 12–15 chief executives from non-competing industries get together for an entire day. All of their organizations are different in size, shape and culture. They listen to a speaker in the morning and in the afternoon share and discuss issues that may be affecting their businesses or themselves personally. It's a chance to bash heads with peers in a completely neutral environment.

My job is to get them to be open and honest so that they can share and collaborate. The concept is a good one, but like most people they can only be open when they feel comfortable, and that is tough when you don't know the person sitting across the table from you. I employ several techniques to break through the nerves. One of the exercises I like to try is called the Trust Walk. I ask everyone to stand up and start mingling. However, there are rules. Each person has to face another person and share one of the four following statements:

We won because we are one. – *Dr Rob Gilbert*

1. I trust you
2. I don't trust you
3. I don't know if I trust you or not
4. I don't care to say.

When they say statements 2–4 what do you think they
are saying? Why don't they trust these people? Trust is
exactly like pregnancy. You either are or you are not. You
either do or you do not. No one has ever been a little bit
pregnant. There is always the discussion – how can I trust
them until I know them? The question they should really
be asking is – why shouldn't I trust them?

In my opinion, trust is over-complicated by years of
cultivating our own personal set of paranoid standards
and beliefs.

Beliefs

The eminent psychologist Dr David Elkins said, 'Research in body and mind medicine is showing that we can support or obstruct our life-force by our beliefs, emotions and behaviour.'

Most of us in our lives have a set of beliefs; some of those beliefs don't work for us today. Let's look at the word 'belief' for a moment. If you were to cross out the B E & F from the word 'belief' – you are left with LIE. Go figure.

I remember my mother taking me to the dentist when I was very young. I remember her saying that it was not going to hurt – it bloody well did. All of a sudden I now had a trust issue with the one person who loved me the most. So imagine being told a few weeks later that we were going to the doctor for an injection. Do you think I was excited about this? My mother had to drag me there, so you can imagine my surprise when I was given a sugar lump!

If you have knowledge, let others light their candles at it.
– Margaret Fuller

So, is it our parents' fault that we have so many trust issues?

Seriously, we all have standards and expectations and sometimes it works for us but more often it works against us. As I have said many times previously, if what you are doing is working, keep doing it. However, I would guess that trust is one of the areas in your life that is not working. Trust is a thorny problem; it is probably one of the easiest tactical issues to handle but without doubt one of the most challenging emotional issues to deal with because of our past experiences.

The events and experiences we have gone through shape who we are but we have to stop allowing them to define us. We have a choice.

E+R=O

It isn't just about how we react to an event, it is how we 'feel' about that event that will shape our outcome and determine how we move forward.

Every event leaves an indelible print on our brain, is added to the memory banks and helps us create our belief structure. For example, a child goes to school and the teacher asks him to volunteer to add up a sum and write the answer on the board. The kid gets it wrong. All the other kids laugh. What do you think the kid says to himself the next time there is a chance to volunteer?

We could change the scenario to a boy asking a girl out or to us losing a client or being turned down for a job we have applied for. Whilst I am not disputing that it is disturbing, it is JUST an event. The way we react and respond to these events will always determine how we feel about the situation. 'So, what has this got to do with trust?' you may be asking yourself. Well, suppose we pluck up the courage to ask that person out or we go for that job and are turned down. We start to mistrust our judgement and our ability to think rationally about what is best for us. As soon as you start down the slippery slope of mistrusting yourself, the rest of the world doesn't stand a chance. We all have doubts and it is natural to question our own behaviour, but we all need balance. We all need to remind ourselves that we can achieve anything so that we continue to believe that we can take risks and win in the end.

It is literally true that you can succeed best and quickest by
helping others to succeed. – *Napoleon Hill*

The real issues behind events are usually incredibly
ordinary and innocent – they only become dramatic in
our mind's eye because of the way it makes us feel. For
example, the fact that you didn't get asked to an interview
for a job would have been about your qualifications and
experience, not about you personally. The girl might have
genuinely had plans and is hoping that the boy will call
her back – meanwhile, he has convinced himself that he
is 'not worthy'.

Things that happen around us are usually nothing to
do with us. When you are knocked back you need to be
honest about why and not allow your emotional response
to rejection or hurt stop you moving forward. You need
to keep trusting your judgement and keep asking difficult
questions to ensure that you make and get the IMPACT
you deserve in the future.

Trust can come in many different forms. What I am
suggesting is, look at what is REALLY in front of you
and not what is behind you. Be in the room and give the
world a chance to support you.

What would you do if you saw a man running towards you with three machete knives in his hand? Personally, I would run like hell because in that moment that is what the situation requires me to do. I would not pause and take a minute to decide whether to trust him or not. I would use my better judgement. Better judgement is the same thing as listening to your gut. As long as you follow your better judgement – which always seems to be plugged into your inner honesty and heart – you will not go far wrong.

What are your trust levels like at the moment?

> 'You have to do it by yourself, and you can't do it alone'
>
> *– Martin Rutte*

Imagine if I did not trust my PA/printer/publisher. How would this book have ever been printed and found its way onto the bookshelves?

In my opinion, 98% of the world conspires to support you. In the workplace, when I am doing training sessions and workshops I get the staff to do a Trust Fall. The process is not really a problem – what is a killer is what we tell ourselves as we put ourselves in the position of trusting our colleagues. Picture this: you are standing on a 6ft high ladder with your back to your colleagues and I ask you to fall back and they will catch you in their arms. Would you trust them?

Or would you tense up? Two per cent of your colleagues may sometimes let you down. Make the decision that if 98% are willing to work and support you – it might be worth trusting the process. Do not set people up to fail so that you can say, 'No wonder...I was right not to trust them.'

My mother has enormous expectations of people and strangely they never quite get it right for her, so she refuses to trust people to get it right in the future. If she set her expectations a little lower she would achieve far more and have what she would consider a successful life. I am not saying you should set your expectations so low that everyone lives up to your poor opinion of them. Instead, you should set your expectations of people realistically and without the interference of your irrational instinct to stay out of harm's way all of the time.

So, getting more IMPACT means allowing people into your world; opening up to vulnerability and empowering your circle of trusted friends and peers to help you achieve your dreams.

There is one other aspect of trust that I would like to share and how it sits with you is your choice. I believe that there is a higher power in existence and it is evident in just about every part of our everyday lives. Even when we have a close shave on the highway or we receive a cheque in the post just in time to clear through the bank ready to pay the bills, we all of us say the same thing (or near enough the same thing): we 'thank heavens' or 'thank God' for looking after us in that moment. As many atheists say it as religious believers. Whatever your religion, you will have your God. If you don't follow a formal religion, you will no doubt live your life to a set of principles and you will set your beliefs against them. We all believe in something.

There is no such thing as a self-made person. You will reach
your goals only with the help of others. – *George Shinn*

At a conference many years ago, a man stood impatiently
waiting for his turn to have a few minutes with the
seminar leader; he became quite noticeable and was very
distracting to the other participants in the room. In order
to keep the peace, Tim Piering, one of the most inspiring
and enlightened men on the planet, intuitively decided
to give this man a quick moment in private before it was
actually his turn. 'You are obviously concerned, sir. How
may I help?' 'Well Tim, I am following everything you're
saying and to tell you the truth I believe everything – ex-
cept – if you keep mentioning this SPIRIT thing, well,
I'm just going to have to leave!'

When Tim asked why, the gentleman replied, 'I don't believe in this God guy or this higher power that you keep
talking about. I believe that we do everything on our own
and we alone are responsible for everything in this world!'

Tim said that he understood how the gentleman felt and
calmly asked him to wait at the side for his proper turn
so that he could get the time that he deserved. Just as the
man agreed to do so, Tim grabbed a rose from a nearby

flower arrangement, handed it to the man and said, 'Oh, by the way, while you're waiting over there, could you make me another one of these flowers?'

The man took the rose, sat down, studied it for a brief moment and then a large wry smile spread across his face when he realized the lesson he had just learned. He leaned over and said, 'Thank you, Tim, I understand!' Then he quietly took his place back in the auditorium and enjoyed the rest of the seminar.

The lesson he learned was that there must be some sort of order, if not an omnipresent power, in the universe. It makes things grow; it guides the changing of the seasons and maybe even humanity. We can't explain everything with science; maybe we should stop trying and just have a little bit of faith.

When you reach out, chances are pretty good that someone will reach back. – *Cheryl Richardson*

Make yourself trust, make yourself believe you can do it

Visualize a 16-foot runway dug out of the ground and filled with red hot white ash from a fire that has been burning for hours. In a moment approximately 12 chief executives are going to walk barefoot across the smouldering embers. Would you make that walk? Would you trust me?

Just before I ask the 12 brave souls to walk on fire I get them to sign waivers just in case of injury. Would you still trust me? Would you make the walk?

Hours earlier I explained how to make the walk without getting hurt, I even get them to practise walking slowly across either a wooden floor or grass patch. I tell them to keep their eyes fixed on the end of the runway, focus on their breathing and enjoy the experience. Yes, enjoy it.

It's a fascinating experience just to watch people live through a fire walk – even when they're just practising on grass. People look down, not ahead. Their breathing gets faster and they start obsessing over the process and start getting really serious. In an instant, trust is lost and they are no longer 'in the room'. So, my job is to bring them back and prove to them that they can do anything if they believe it.

Getting that through to people is not that difficult, it just feels like a really big deal to them when they are living inside panic and mistrust. In another exercise, I use a wooden hunting arrow, which I place on the softest part of their neck, I ask them to think of a BHAG (big, hairy, audacious goal) and then 'lean towards the risk'. They break the arrow without hurting themselves – which is always a relief. This simple act gives them the confidence to trust me, but more importantly to trust themselves and to recognize what they fear or what they want instead of the fear. The arrow was never going to paralyse them, but their fear did a pretty good job. It is a liberating experience.

> We do not believe if we do not live and work
> according to our belief. – *Heidi Wills*

When we fly, we trust the pilot. When we turn on the electricity we trust that it will work. Sometimes we don't need all the answers, we just need to trust the process.

In my opinion, the world conspires to help us, provided it knows what we want.

We need to put ourselves out into the universe and trust the process.

Look at people in a new light; trust them until they let you down, but don't set them up for failure.

Trust yourself

When married couple Debra and Andrew Veal entered
the 3,000 mile Ward Evans Atlantic Rowing Challenge,
they believed that their profound knowledge of each
other would give them the edge over the other – mainly
male – competitors. Yet during their first night in open
waters, they were confronted with a discovery that would
leave their transatlantic bid in tatters: Andrew, an experienced rower, was suffering from an uncontrollable fear
of the ocean. Try as they might to overcome this, by day
eight, Andrew's distress had become unbearable for both
of them. After a night of soul-searching, Andrew reso-
lutely decided to give up.

Debra could have bowed out of the race fearing she
couldn't complete it without her husband and team-mate,
but she was relishing the journey and wanted to see how
far she could go as a solo-rower. Word of Debra's adven-
ture led to international press coverage and she received
thousands of text messages from well-wishers who were

We define ourselves by the best that is in us, not the worst
that has been done to us. – *Edward Lewis*

keenly following her progress. After 112 days, Debra completed the voyage and landed in Barbados.

Do you think Debra trusted herself? What would you have done? Would you have given up or trusted your inner voice that said 'you can do it'?

Whenever you want to make an IMPACT there will be lots of people who will say it will never happen. People say things because they are afraid and they don't want you to succeed where they doubt they could. Just look over some of the comments these people have made.

'Computers in the future may weigh no more than 1.5 tons.'
                                    – *Popular Mechanics, 1949.*

'I think there is a world market for maybe five computers.'
                    – *Thomas Watson, Chairman of IBM, 1943.*

'I have travelled the length and breadth of this country and talked with the best people, and I can

assure you that data processing is a fad that won't
last out the year.'
  — *The editor in charge of business books for Prentice*
Hall, 1957.

'But what is it good for?'
  — *Engineer at the Advanced Computing Systems Division*
of IBM, 1968, commenting on the microchip.

'There is no reason anyone would want a computer
in their home.'
  — *Ken Olson, President, Chairman and Founder of*
Digital Equipment Corporation, 1977.

'This telephone has too many shortcomings to be
seriously considered as a means of communication.
The device is inherently of no value to us.'
  — *Western Union internal memo, 1876.*

'The wireless music box has no imaginable
commercial value. Who would pay for a message
sent to nobody in particular?'
  — *David Sarnoff's associates in response to his urgings*
for investment in the radio in the 1920s.

One day, in retrospect, the years of struggle will strike you as
the most beautiful. – *Sigmund Freud*

'The concept is interesting and well-formed, but in order to earn better than a C, the idea must be feasible.'
— *A Yale University management professor in response to Fred Smith's paper proposing reliable overnight delivery service (Smith went on to found Federal Express).*

'Who wants to hear actors talk?'
— *H. M. Warner, Warner Brothers, 1927.*

'A Cookie Store is a bad idea. Besides, the market research report says America like crispy cookies, not soft and chewy cookies like you make.'
— *Response to Debbie Fields' idea of starting Mrs Fields Cookies.*

'We don't like their sound, and guitar music is on the way out.'
— *Decca Recording Co rejecting the Beatles, 1962.*

'Everything that can be invented, has been invented.'
— *Charles H. Duell, Commissioner US Office of Patents, 1899.*

'640K ought to be enough (RAM) for anybody.'
                                          – Bill Gates, 1981.

If you don't think you can make an IMPACT, think
about the people behind these comments and what they
went on to achieve. They firmly believed in their own
ability and carried on despite being engulfed by tidal
wave of negativity. So, no matter what you are doing, if
it seems that you aren't getting any closer to your goals or
creating enough IMPACT, just pause for a moment and
before you quit think about these people.

After Fred Astaire's first screen test, the memo sent from
the testing director of MGM, dated 1933, said, 'Can't act!
Slightly bald! Can dance a little!' Astaire kept that memo
over the fireplace in his Beverley Hills home.

Beethoven handled the violin awkwardly and preferred
playing his own compositions instead of improving his
technique. His teacher called him 'hopeless' as a com-
poser.

Charles Darwin, father of the Theory of Evolution, gave
up a medical career and was told by his father, 'You care

Let us live out of our imagination instead of our memory.
                                          – Les Brown

for nothing but shooting, dogs and rat catching.' In his autobiography, Darwin wrote, 'I was considered by all my masters and by my father, a very ordinary boy, rather below the common standard in intellect.'

Walt Disney was fired by a newspaper editor for lack of ideas; he also went bankrupt several times before he built Disneyland.

Thomas Edison's teachers said he was too stupid to learn anything.

Albert Einstein did not speak until he was four years old and didn't read until he was seven. His teacher described him as 'mentally slow, unsociable and adrift forever in his foolish dreams'. He was expelled and was refused admittance to the Zurich Polytechnic School.

Winston Churchill failed sixth grade. He did not become Prime Minister of England until he was 62, and then only after a lifetime of defeats and setbacks. His greatest contributions came when he was a 'senior citizen'.

Richard Branson left school at the age of 15.

Alan Sugar left school at age 16.

Eighteen publishers turned down Richard Bach's 10,000 word story about a 'soaring' gull – *Jonathan Livingston Seagull* – before Macmillan finally published it in 1970. By 1975 it had sold more than seven million copies in the US alone.

YOU CAN DO IT!

As we grow older, we discover that we have two hands: One for helping ourselves, the second for helping others.
– *Unknown*

Exercise

Write down your deepest desire and share it with your closest ally. Take heart from their support.

Write down what you want to achieve this week and ask for help. Trust your 'team' to help you with even the most sensitive issues on your list this week.

Visualize your success and tell yourself that you can do it. Repeat this process over and over again. Use this pleasant image to help you focus when things are going badly.

CHAPTER SEVEN

The Impact Code

What next?

Keeping the Code alive

Keeping the Code alive

Well, you made it to the end. Well done.

Now comes the hard bit: actually putting the IMPACT Code into practice. You will probably have to read the book again to really take it in, but let's summarize what we have talked about.

The IMPACT Code is as much about how you think as it is about what you do. However, thought without action is a pointless waste of life. You need to start really caring for yourself as well as others and make giving to both yourself and others part of your everyday living. It is only by creating positive IMPACT in other people's lives that you will create the IMPACT you so deeply crave in your own life.

The universe is perfectly balanced; it rewards effort with results. Unfortunately, inactivity does not generate nothing; it leaves your life open to other people to change and influence it. Where there is a void, someone will fill it. Make sure you control what fills your life.

> Trust yourself, you know far more than you think you do.
> – Dr Benjamin Spock

The life lessons here centre around being true to yourself and loving yourself enough to live up to your dreams. Only you have the power to create a good life for yourself and consequently, only you can make the changes necessary to affect your life. No matter how grand your dreams are they are still worth chasing; the journey matters more than crossing the finishing line. The real joy is often trying not winning – although it is pretty darned fantastic when you do win! You can't argue with that.

What really matters is that you make a commitment to yourself to put your own life right. Stop blaming, stop whining and get on with building a better life. Bitching about life won't make it better. I had a brief fling with that in the past and I can assure you it doesn't work.

If you find it hard to change the way you think, then find yourself a good role model and start copying the way they live and act. Remember…FAKE IT TILL YOU MAKE IT! There is no shame in needing a frame of reference for success. You may not have any experience in how to make your dreams a reality, so learn from the best. In time you won't need to think about it; in time someone may be copying your behaviour. Stranger things have happened.

Open your heart. Allow yourself to be vulnerable. TELL THE TOTAL TRUTH FASTER. Your friends and family will love you all the more for it. Nobody decent laughs at anyone who is prepared to have a go and live for their dreams. Try your best to put fear of failure aside and take a positive step 'into the room'. It will feel great and the results will amaze you. Even the smallest change can create phenomenal IMPACT.

Ask for help. Get a Mastermind team in place to help you realize your dreams. I am here to support you – all you have to do is ask. Remember…

> 'You have to do it by yourself, and you can't do it alone.'
>
> – *Martin Rutte*

Remember, nobody is worth sacrificing yourself for – not even your kids. There is always a way to get what you want; it might take longer but the compromise should never be yourself. Nobody wants a wasted life on their conscience – especially your kids.

When you have confidence, you can have a lot of fun. And when you have fun, you can do amazing things. – *Joe Namath*

Never stop learning and never stop asking questions, but most importantly, never stop believing that you deserve the life you dream about.

If you can dream about it, you can do it.

But, perhaps the most important point is this: when you are in the room, be in the room.

A lot of the IMPACT Code will naturally fall into place when you adopt a different approach to being 'present'. Yes, make your plans. Yes, share your dreams. Yes, give as well as take. But be PRESENT in all that you do.

Please also note that there is no order to the Code. You don't have to implement one aspect of the Code before you can move onto another. This is a way of living, not a set of rigid rules.

Have fun with your life, with the journey – the good times and the bad times. Keep asking yourself, 'If I'm not having fun, why am I doing it?' If you have got a good answer as to why you are doing something you don't particularly enjoy, then fine; if not, stop doing it.

It is your job to make life palatable – not every aspect of your life will be a roaring blast of fun and high energy, but drudgery is often where you find nobility. Maybe you need to do the things you dislike to keep your family safe. Don't give up because you have no choice; take heart that even the bad days are taking you where you want to go. If you can't find why you are doing something then you aren't being true to yourself about what you really want and what you truly have to do to achieve it. All the best things in life are worth working for and anything worth a jot is worth waiting for.

Living a life that is dominated by the desire to create IMPACT for you and everyone around you will set you free.

'It's never too late to be the person you could have been.'

– George Eliot

Surround yourself with people who believe you can.
– Dan Zadra

Six ways to keep the IMPACT Code alive

- Every day – watch yourself in the room.
- Every week – ask yourself 'on whom did I make an IMPACT?'
- Every year – spend a day looking at who reduces your IMPACT or fills your life with negative energy. Determine to take action to reduce their IMPACT on your life.
- Ask your three closest friends if you have added value to your friendship in the past year. Devise ways to make a difference from now on.
- Look at people through trusting eyes.
- Celebrate actions you have taken to get your life on track.

The IMPACT Poem

Is anybody happier because you passed their way,
Does anyone remember that you spoke with them today.
Were you selfish pure and simple as you rushed
along your way,
Or is someone mighty grateful for a deed you did today.

Can you say tonight in passing with the day that's
slipping past,
That you helped a single human in the many that
you passed.
Is a single heart rejoicing over what you did or said,
Can a person whose hopes were fading now with
courage look ahead.

Imagination is the preview of life's coming attractions.
— *Larry Eisenberg*

Did you waste a day or lose it, was it well or poorly spent,
Did you leave a trail of kindness or a scar of discontent.
When you close your eyes in slumber, do you think
your God will say,
You have earned one more tomorrow for the deeds
you did today.

– Max Hutching

More words of wisdom

'Until you actually make a physical move and take action, all the dreaming and scheming in the world will get you nowhere near your vision.'

— Pat Croce

'The act of taking the first step is what separates the winners from the losers.'

— Brian Tracy

'Vision without action is a daydream.
Action without vision is a nightmare.'

— Japanese proverb

'When it comes to getting things done, we need fewer architects and more bricklayers.'

— Colleen Barrett

'The great end of life is not knowledge but action.'

— Thomas Huxley

We are all born originals – why is it so many of us die copies?
– Edward Young

'As I grow older, I pay less attention to what men say. I just watch what they do.'

— Andrew Carnegie

'I think one's feelings waste themselves in words; they ought all to be distilled into actions which bring results.'

— Florence Nightingale

'What you do speak so loudly that I cannot hear what you say.'

— Ralph Waldo Emerson

'We cannot do everything at once, but we can do something at once.'

— Calvin Coolidge

'There are risks and costs to a programme of action but they are far less than the long-range risks and costs of comfortable inaction.'

— John F. Kennedy

'We make a living by what we get, but we make a
life by what we give.'

– Winston Churchill

'If you don't know where you're going, any road will
take you there.'

– Proverb

'Compelling Trust is the highest form of human
motivation.'

– Stephen R. Covey

'No dream is too extreme.'

– Walt Disney's Pinocchio

'The ultimate measure of a man is not where he
stands in moments of comfort, but where he stands
at times of challenge.'

– Martin Luther King, Jr.

'Blessed are those who can give without
remembering and take without forgetting.'

– Elizabeth Bibesco

Time invested in improving ourselves cuts down on time
wasted in disapproving of others. – Leona Green

'We work to become, not to acquire.'
                                    – *Elbert Hubbard*

'May you live every day of your life.'
                                    – *Jonathan Swift*

'If I take care of my character, my reputation will take care of me.'
                                    – *Dwight L. Moody*

'Vision is the art of seeing things invisible.'
                                    – *Jonathan Swift*

'Give more and you'll have more.'
                                    – *Hyrum W. Smith*

'She was never conscious of my limitations.'
                                    – *Helen Keller (tribute to Anne Sullivan)*

'Life is one great big canvas; throw all the paint on it you can.'
                                    – *Danny Kaye*

'Change always comes bearing gifts.'

> *– Price Pritchett*

'Do not follow where the path may lead. Go instead where there is no path and leave a trail.'

> *– Muriel Strode*

'To reach any significant goal, you must leave your comfort zone.'

> *– Hyrum W. Smith*

'We cling to our own point of view, as though everything depended on it. Yet our opinions have no permanence; like autumn and winter, they gradually pass away.'

> *Chuang Tzu*

Bury your ego. Don't be the star. Be the star maker!
– Bud Hadfield

More exercises

In the room

Ask yourself…

- But now where am I?
- Is this a place I chose, or was it chosen for me?
- How often do I give 100% attention?
- How often do I wish I was somewhere else?
- Am I listening or waiting to respond?
- Am I living in the present or blaming the past?
- Am I living all my todays with passion or waiting till it feels right?

Modelling

- Who are your heroes?
- Why are they your heroes?
- What do they do that you admire?
- What one Action have you modelled in the last 21 days?
- Fake it till you make it.

- Act as if…
- What do you need to do to step up a gear?
- Do you want a Mastermind team?
- Who do you know that would be interested?
- Do you need support setting one up?
- You might want to read my book on Masterminding…

Passion

- Am I living my passion?
- What excites me?
- This is not a dress rehearsal for the rest of your life so are you doing or starting the process of living a life you deserve?

To help you find your purpose ask yourself the following questions:

- What do I believe in?
- In what guiding principles can I become constructively obsessed?
- What governs my life?
- What do I stand for?
- What puts meaning in my life?

There is no such thing as expecting too much.
– *Susan Cheever*

- What qualities are important for my life to be complete?

Action

- What have you done today to CREATE the life you want?
- Over the last 21 days how many times have you put off doing the things that might be uncomfortable?
- If five birds are sitting on a wire and one of them decides to fly, how many birds would be left on the wire? (This is the big question. The answer is still five – making a decision to fly without acting on the decision is a waste of energy.)
- Put the C into
      INNOVATION (INNOV ACTION)
      INSPIRATION (INSPIR ACTION)
      MOTIVATION (MOTIV ACTION)
  and then the magic will happen…

'There is no try; you do or you don't.'
      – *Yoda, Jedi Master and kick-ass philosopher*

Comic relief

- When did you last have a belly laugh?
- What funny films or TV programmes have you watched recently?
- How can you see the funny side to some of your past experiences?
- Is the group you hang around with funny? If not, find some new friends.
- Go to a comedy club every six months.
- Make a point of looking for humour everywhere you go.

Trust

- Who is in your circle of trust?
- What do you know is the truth?
- Are you sure it's the truth?
- Could you trust more?
- Do people let you down?
- Are your expectations too high?
- What standards and beliefs do you use to trust people?
- Are these beliefs working for or against you moving forward?

Caring is the ultimate competitive advantage.
– *Ron Kendrick*

Solutions to the dot puzzles

9 dot puzzle

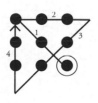

16 dot puzzle

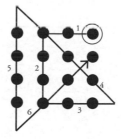

Further reading

Anyone Can Do It, Sahar Hashemi

Sumo, Paul McGee

Walking Tall, Lesley Everett

African Wisdom, Steff Du Plessis

The Power of Focus: How to Hit Your Business and Financial Targets with Absolute Certainty, Jack Canfield, Mark Victor Hansen, and Les Hewitt. Deerfield Beach, Fla. Health Communications 2000

The Aladdin Factor: How to Ask and Get Anything You Want in Life, Jack Canfield and Mark Victor Hansen. New York: Berkley 1995

Think and Grow Rich, Napoleon Hill. New York: Fawcett Crest 1960

The 7 Habits of Highly Effective People, Stephen R. Covey New York Fireside 1989

The Traits of Champions: The Secrets to Championship Performance in Business, Golf and Life, Andrew Wood and Brian Tracy. Provo, Utah: Executive Excellence Publishing 2000

Unlimited Power, Anthony Robbins. New York: Simon & Schuster 1986

The Magic of Thinking Big, David Schwartz. New York: Fireside 1987

50 Success Classics, Tom Butler-Bowden. Yarmouth Maine: Nicholas Brealey Publishing 2004

The E-Myth Revisited: Why Most Small Businesses Don't Work and What to Do About it, Michael Gerber. New York: Harper Business 1995

The One Minute Manager, Kenneth Blanchard and Spencer Johnson. New York: Berkley Books 1983

Built to Last: The Successful Habits of Visionary Companies, Jim Collins and Jerry I. Porras. New York: Harper Business 1997

Good to Great: Why Some Companies Make the Leap...and Others Don't, Jim Collins. New York: Harper Business 2001

Chicken Soup for the Soul, Jack Canfield and Mark Victor Hansen. Deerfield Beach, Florida; Florida Health Communications 1993

The Four Agreements: A Practical Guide to Personal Freedom, Don Miguel Ruiz. San Rafael, California: Amber-Allen 1999

*Don't Sweat the Small Stuff...*and *It's All Small Stuff:*
Simple Ways to Keep the Little Things from Taking Over
Your Life, Richard Carlson. New York: Hyperion 1997

Life Strategies: Doing What Works, Doing What Matters,
Philip C. McGraw PhD. New York: Hyperion 1999

The Seven Spiritual Laws of Success, Deepak Chopra. San
Rafael, California: Amber-Allen 1994

About Nigel Risner

The only motivational speaker in Europe to have been awarded Speaker of the Year from both The Academy of Chief Executives and The Executive Committee, Nigel is a respected author, television presenter and prolific speaker. He speaks with authority: his own life having veered perilously away from comfortable norms at times. He has learned that positive results can come from negative experiences and that we often learn best from situations which are unfamiliar and even uncomfortable.

As one of the youngest CEOs of a financial services company in the City of London, Nigel knows business as well as he knows life and more importantly he knows what it takes to lead a successful business! Unlike other speakers or consultants, he has the ability to translate – with electrifying effect – that hands on experience into a coherent, compelling and exciting philosophy, which has made him one of Europe's leading speakers and a powerful professional coach to some of the world's leading business executives.

Today he conducts more than 150 seminars and speeches a year for an enormous variety of companies and organizations in Britain and overseas. When he isn't travelling, Nigel lives with his wife and two children in Hertfordshire.

Why not invite Nigel to come into your organization and help transform your results with the IMPACT Code? For more information contact Nigel on nigel@nigelrisner.com

www.nigelrisner.com

Praise for Nigel

'I am writing to thank you for helping me "let go". I did as agreed and sat down with both my parents and asked them how they felt about me. Were they proud of me, etc. Initially they were a little surprised, then saddened that I did not already know how extremely proud of me they were, not only as their daughter but as a person. As you can probably imagine it was a little emotional for everyone, but it did open up a long overdue conversation about what each of us think of one another. Thus, on behalf of my family I thank you deeply for changing my life – I have never been so truly happy.'

– Dr Karen Pugh

'I first saw Nigel speak in early 2001 and I can honestly say that it changed my life. Since then we have used Nigel as a speaker many times at company

events and he has always been a 100% success.
Nigel's message is clear, honest and uplifting. By
taking responsibility yourself you can turn your
year into a great year rather than just another year.
Definitely read the IMPACT code, but do not finish
with it, keep it as a point of reference for the years
ahead.'

    — Mark Dixon, Group Managing Director, WYKO

'I can say without fear that yesterday morning was
and will be the most valuable three hours of my
working life in recent years, if not ever!'

                             — Ali Stronach, WYKO

'You have changed my life! I've been going through
a very difficult time with the restructuring within
our company and it feels as though I have reached
the end of my career at this company. You have
made my outlook more positive and one thing I will
always remember and try to practise everyday: 'If
you're in the room, be in the room.'

                                    — Diana Kruger

'YOU made the difference and wow! What a fantastic day it was! The energy in the room was buzzing and I know this was in part down to the effort and enthusiasm YOU put into making your session an unforgettable experience.'
— *Kriss Akabussi MBE, The Akabussi Company*

'Nigel is the best speaker I know. I love listening to him; he is entertaining, thought-provoking and always leaves you with a life-changing thought. Every time I have heard him speak he has new and fantastic content, I would not hesitate to recommend Nigel, you will love him.'
— *Penny Power, Founder and Director, Ecademy Limited*

'Without getting too deep and heavy you have now not only once, but twice, inspired me. After Wednesday, I took time that night to rewind what all you had said and came up with the following statement and I do believe this is my passion. "TO LIVE MY LIFE AS A BANK ACCOUNT" to constantly make deposits into other people's lives (as you have done in mine) so that the interest accrued will supersede any withdrawal I may ever need to make.'
— *Craig Kater*

'Nigel is a positive, warm and enthusiastic person who is genuinely out to help you. If you never get to hear Nigel speak, you have missed out.'

– Graham Jones

'Nigel is a very inspirational speaker. You won't need motivating to get along to one of his motivational speeches – just do it!'

– Martin Watt

Other titles by Nigel Risner

- *You Had Me At Hello: The New Rules for Better Networking*

- *It's a Zoo Around Here! The New Rules for Better Communication*

- *The Magic of Masterminding: The New Rules for Better Goal Setting*

Risner's Reminders:
- *10 Steps to Becoming an Effective Leader*
- *10 Steps to Becoming Personally Empowered*
- *10 Steps to Effective Time Management*
- *10 Steps to Getting What you Deserve*

- *10 Steps to Reaching Your Goals*
- *10 Traits to Highly Successful People*

Audio-visual tools for self-development:
- *Moments of Truth* set of 12 audio CDs
- *Self Mastery for Your Personal Success* video, audio (3 cassettes or 2 CDs) and workbook

To order any of these titles or to find out more information about the complete range of services available from Nigel Risner visit our website. If you would like to receive Nigel's FREE weekly e-zine visit our website and register today.

www.nigelrisner.com

Index